The Fishmonger

About the Author

Born in Cork, Pat O'Connell comes from a family steeped in business tradition on both sides. He was educated at Coláiste Chríost Rí Cork and at Cork Regional Technical College, from which he graduated in Business Studies. After working as an official with Cork Corporation, he took up employment at his mother's fish stall, Kay O'Connell Fish Merchants, in the English Market in Cork. Today, in partnership with his brother Paul, he runs the award-winning fish stall as well as an oak-burning smokehouse in Bandon. An active member of the Market Traders Association, Cork Business Association, Good Food Ireland and Retail Excellence Ireland, Pat became famous all around the globe when a photograph of him laughing with Queen Elizabeth II became one of the most iconic images of the monarch's historic state visit to the Republic of Ireland in 2011.

The Fishmonger

Pat O'Connell

The Liffey Press

Published by
The Liffey Press Ltd
Raheny Shopping Centre, Second Floor
Raheny, Dublin 5, Ireland
www.theliffeypress.com

A catalogue record of this book is
available from the British Library.

ISBN 978-1-908308-50-4

Edited by Patricia Ahern

Printed in Spain by GraphyCems.

Contents

Foreword

He runs one of the most successful fish businesses in Ireland, and when, in May 2011, he made Queen Elizabeth II roar with laughter, he also became something of an international figure. It isn't surprising, therefore, that Pat O'Connell's warm and honest memoir does much more than simply tell his life story – *The Fishmonger* is also a social history.

At the heart of Pat's story is his family's extraordinary, fifty-year connection with the English Market in Cork. He begins by explaining how, in 1963, his mother flouted tradition by taking over her own fish stall in the market. Pat describes a wooden table and marble slab top fitted with rainwater gutters, as well as an old, grey, hang-up scales and a painted plywood sign. As Pat so simply remarks, 'In no time at all she was up and running.' And from this modest beginning she, and later Paul and Pat, built up their highly-acclaimed fish business. It is only too easy to forget, in this age of relatively equal opportunity, how difficult it was for women to establish themselves in a career, especially when they were married and had children. Pat paints an intriguing picture of his mother, Kay, clearly an exceptionally intelligent and strong-minded woman, as well as his other family members.

Pat's family history and the history of their business are, of course, interwoven with the history of the English Market. Pat shares his encyclopaedic knowledge of the market and places it in the wider context of trading in Cork city and in Ireland over the last half-century. He compares the original fish market (fish has been sold on the site continuously for over four hundred years) and points out that, in some ways, little has really changed in all that time. In describing the market's past – not to mention its ability to survive endless adversity, including fire, famine, recession, revolution and, most dangerous of all, renovation – he also explains how the market is inextricably linked with the rise and fall of the social, economic and cultural life of the city. This is not, strictly speaking, a political book, and yet it deftly deals with food and local politics in the widest meaning of the term.

In describing his mother's formidable discipline, hard work, entrepreneurship and incredible energy, one suspects that Pat might also be describing himself. Having observed Pat at work in the market, it would be no exaggeration to describe him as a powerhouse. Before commending to you this highly enjoyable and instructive read, I should also add that *The Fishmonger* is packed full of anecdotes. Indeed, Pat reveals exactly why Queen Elizabeth II warmed to him so publicly. It isn't, as you'll understand when you have read this book, so very surprising that he should win over royalty. He has the same effect on almost everyone he meets.

Rebecca Harte
Farmgate Café, Cork
October 2013

To my parents Kathleen and John who worked selflessly and tirelessly to provide Paul and myself with a better life.

'If I have seen further, it is by standing on the shoulders of giants.' – Isaac Newton

Prologue

About 11.00 a.m., we packed the main counters with ice and began to put our display together. This was very much Paul's responsibility as he has a wonderful eye for arranging fish and colour, which is probably why he is such a great photographer. My job had been to source the fish. Paul's job was to display it. Over the next few hours, under the watchful eye of Paul, everyone worked together to create a really stunning array of local, fresh fish, mostly from Castletownbere, all fit for a queen and displayed in a fashion to make the rest of the world envious of the bounty we have surrounding this island of ours: huge prawns, beautiful turbot, hake, lemon sole, plaice, mackerel, oysters, live crab and lobster, haddock, gurnard, monkfish and whiting. We topped it all off with lovely wild salmon from the River Lee and organic salmon from Bantry.

At this stage, the market was buzzing, with the stall holders fussing and double checking to make sure everything was shipshape. Bord Bia were giving advice to stall holders on final tweaks to the displays. Everywhere, cameras were flashing. The sense of anticipation was palpable. RTÉ were busy getting cameras into position, with the lighting having been put in the

1

previous week. Security personnel were hovering around in large numbers, scrutinising every single detail.

About 1.00 p.m., RTÉ did a practice walk through the route the queen would take, to make sure that their camera angles and lighting were correct. They had to get it right as they were the feed for the other television stations showing the event and their coverage was going out worldwide. For the trial run, one of their producers, Marie Toft, picked the short straw to play the part of the queen. Accompanied by the lord mayor and several others, she followed the official route the queen would take in less than an hour. The group stopped at each of the stalls the queen would visit and tried to imitate the walk-through as best they could. Marie played the part of the queen to perfection, or at least it matched my perception of what the queen would be like – very formal, very straitlaced, aloof, without any sense of humour. If the real queen was indeed like this, my Cork wit and irreverence would go down like a lead balloon. Later, I tried to speak to one of the producers, to spell out my concerns, but it was impossible to get near any of the crew at this stage, as they were run off their feet. So, what should I do – go frightfully formal or Cork cheeky?

1

The Quiet One

Our family was steeped in business on both sides, back through the generations. Yet, when I was young, going into the family business full-time was the last thing on my mind.

Mam always worked outside the home, even after she married, which was rare in those times. When I was born in Cork in 1957, Mam went back to work soon afterwards, cleaning houses three days a week in the city suburbs of Blackrock and Shanakiel. Even to this day, I still have nasty memories of climbing up the steep hill with her to Shanakiel. One day, I stopped on the Shaky Bridge, plonked myself down and insisted that I could walk no further. But Mam had a way of getting around me and kept cajoling me until I eventually got up and carried on. As well as cleaning houses, Mam also worked behind the counter for a day and a half at McCarthy's fish stall in the English Market, which is an old, indoor food market in the heart of Cork city, run by Cork City Council, with a variety of rented stalls and entrances from Patrick Street, the Grand Parade, Princes Street and Oliver Plunkett Street. At the time, the stall holders sold mainly fresh fish, poultry and vegetables. Dad worked with Cork Corporation as a road sweeper. Later, he became a truck driver in the cleansing department and also a shop steward with the Irish Transport and General Workers' Union.

As long as I can remember, I have always been called Pat or Patrick. Yet I was christened Gerard. Apparently, a neighbour of ours on the back Douglas Road where I was born kept asking my mother, 'How is Juddy?' This infuriated my mother so much that she changed my name to Patrick. In our family, changing names seemed to be common, as my dad was christened Patrick John and was called Paddy by his workmates, but everyone else, including my Mam, called him John. In hindsight, it's probably no wonder I've been confused all my life.

For the first few years of my childhood, we lived in a little cottage near the church at Turner's Cross, at the edge of the city. Dad's family lived nearby in a high, red-brick terraced house on Evergreen Road – his parents, whom I called Nan and Pop, along with their son Paul, their daughters Noreen and Rosie and Rosie's daughter Imelda.

When I was three years old, we moved to a three-bedroom bungalow in Friar's Walk, which had lovely gardens and was still within walking distance of my grandparents' house. From then on, all of Dad's wages went on paying the mortgage, which meant we had to live on Mam's earnings.

Just below our house, Cork Corporation had a storage yard and it was there in front of the yard that Dad learned to drive a dumper. Raising myself up on my toes, I stood at our front window and watched his every move as he drove slowly along, tipped the big, heavy skip and then carefully hoisted it up again. I felt so proud of him.

Every few weeks, Dad went for a haircut to Connie Long's on Barrack Street. Before moving to Evergreen Road, Dad and his parents had lived across the road from Connie in Crowley's Lane, so Connie and Dad were good friends. Whenever Dad went for a haircut, he took me along too, as Connie usually gave two trims for the price of one. Before taking the scissors to me, Connie placed a big board between the arms of a chair, then lifted me up and landed me down right in the centre, in front of a big mirror. 'Now Pat, stay as still as you can,' he'd say to me, giving me a gentle pat on the shoulder. So much for health and safety! Connie's customers never minded waiting, as they always chatted away and caught up with all the local sport. With passion, they replayed matches from start to finish, slated referees for wrong decisions, named their man of the match, picked the team for the next game, sized up the opposition and proudly recalled the skills of great sporting heroes of the past, such as Christy Ring and Jack Lynch. Being at the barber's was a social outing for the lot of them and they relished every minute of their time there. After every trip to Connie's, Dad told Mam about all the men we had met and spoke about Connie as if he was the best barber in Ireland.

While Mam and Dad were at work, our neighbour Mrs Casey looked after me, or Nan and Pop. Like Dad, Pop had worked with Cork Corporation. But when he hurt his back there, he had to give up. He never again worked and I remember him being around the house a lot.

When I started at the South Presentation convent in Douglas Street, Pop took on the task of collecting me each day after school. Sometimes, if the weather was good, he'd say, 'We'll go for a nice walk today Pat.' Then, he'd take my school bag and, hand in hand, we'd stroll along at our ease. On the way, he'd stop off at a shop and stock up on a few loose Sweet Afton cigarettes, or Woodbines. Then, we'd continue our stroll.

Pop liked his pint and, more often than not, we ended up in a pub known as Celia's Bar or in the Silver Goblet, where he'd treat me to a glass of raspberry and a packet of Perry crisps, while he took his time over a few pints of stout. Before ordering his last pint, he'd say, 'Just one for the road so.' I always came out of the bar with a big, red, raspberry moustache. But Pop never seemed to notice, maybe because by then he was always a little merry. On the way home, he'd stop all of a sudden, bend down and say to me, 'Pat, listen, whatever you do, don't tell Nan where we've been.' Then, he'd straighten himself up, put his finger to his lips and I'd do the same. But, Nan was no fool. The minute she'd see us, she'd look Pop straight in the eye and say, 'You've been to the pub and taken that poor innocent child with you. Shame on you!' But, he never took any notice and always pretended not to hear her. Rubbing his two hands together, he'd say, 'We're starving.' Then, he'd open the press, take out a fresh loaf of white bread, cut two thick slices for the two of us and toast them on a fork by the fire. 'Pull up to the table there Pat,' he'd say to me and he'd coat the crunchy toast in butter.

Nan never got cross with me, except once, while I was on holiday with her in Crosshaven, where she rented a house every summer at Graball Bay. One day, unknown to her, I took off with a pal and went exploring around the seashore and cliffs. She searched high and low for me and got into a right state worrying about me. We didn't come back for a few hours and she nearly murdered me when I appeared. But she never complained about me to Mam. Instead, when we got home, she praised me to the hilt and told Mam that I'd been the best boy ever.

Nan was a busy woman and ran a shop on Barrack Street, selling fresh meat. She got her supplies from two nearby bacon factories, Murphy's on Evergreen Road and Lunham's, just off Dunbar Street, where my aunt Noreen once worked. Often, when Nan and Rosie drove to the factories to pick up boxes of meat, they took me along too. Murphy's in particular was a bit gruesome. It was very noisy, with squealing pigs, and the pigs could be seen being sliced down the middle. I have vague memories of pigs passing through some sort of furnace.

Just like Nan, Mam's mother was a businesswoman. She kept lorries for hire, which were driven by her sons, who were all much older than Mam. Also, she ran a pub, the Laurel Bar in Mary Street, and lived overhead. She also owned a vegetable shop on George's Quay, which sold some fish on a Friday. At that time, several small boats fished down by Blackrock Castle and landed their catch on George's Quay, so it made sense to sell some fish in the shop. Mam ran the vegetable shop for her mother for many years, until she married Dad. Maybe having charge of that shop gave Mam the urge to want her own business. The fact that she was the only girl in a family of seven boys may have driven her on too.

In 1963, just a year after my brother Paul was born, Mam got the chance to set up on her own when the Mortell family gave up their fish stall in the English Market. The stall took up an area of about 120 square feet, at a side wall near the Grand Parade exit. Mam decided to rent it and gave up her cleaning jobs, as well as her job at McCarthy's fish stall. She bought a wooden table and an old, grey hang-up scales from Russell's provisions shop on Prince's Street, in a closing-down sale, as well as a few rolls of wallpaper from Water's paint and wall-paper shop. Dad picked up a marble slab for her to use as a counter and he fitted rainwater gutters around the table top, to take the water run-off. Her cousin Jack Keating, a painter, printed her name on a sheet of plywood to hang over the stall. In no time at all, she was up and running.

Dad and his family were fully behind her. But a few fish traders in the market were not at all happy and put up much resistance. They frowned upon the fact that somebody who had been an employee of another stall was now becoming a stall holder and a competitor. I have no doubt they also suspected that she was a bit of a tough cookie and had the potential to be serious competition. The fact that she was a woman annoyed them too. At the time, most of the women who ran stalls in the market were widows who had taken over the business from their late husbands, or women from families with a long tradition of trading there. Mam was a newcomer, a blow-in, and she wasn't wanted. But that didn't put her off. If anything, it drove her on all the more.

Yet it was a huge gamble for her, especially as there were already about thirteen fish stalls in the market, as well as many around the city, such as Quain's on Prince's Street and Mc-Curtain Street, Williams' on Oliver Plunkett Street, and Larry Couche's on Parliament Street. All of them were well established, whereas Mam was starting from scratch. At the time, Catholics held steadfast to the practice of not eating meat on a Friday and eating fish instead. But, apart from Thursday and Friday, sales of fish were usually low. Looking back on it now, going into the fish business might seem to have been a bad choice. But times were different then. People had fewer demands and lived on less.

From the time Mam took over the stall, our family life changed big time. Before that, Mam had stayed at home with us every morning until it was time to take me to school. Running a fish shop meant that she had to rise at about 6.00 a.m. most mornings to make the fish auctions in the city, as they started around 7.00 a.m. At the time, all the fish stalls in the market closed at weekends and took a half day on Wednesdays. In the city, the fish auctions were held at two locations, one in Clayton Love on Cornmarket Street and the other on Alfred Street, near the railway station.

Usually, I went along to the auctions with Mam. Hauling fish back from Albert Street to the market by trolley could be a nightmare, especially as we were often delayed by a goods train that ran from the railway station, through Albert Street, over the bridges and on towards City Hall. Mostly, we bought at Clayton Love, as it was the nearest auction to the English Market. A big, long wide building, with plenty of room for delivery trucks to drive in and out, it ran parallel to Castle Street, from Cornmarket Street right through to North Main Street.

One side of the building had glass panelling and stored groceries for the wholesalers, while the other side was used for the fish auctions. Timber boxes of fish lined the floor. The supplies came mainly from Ballycotton, Union Hall and Crosshaven. All boxes of fish were weighed and tagged on arrival. They consisted mostly of whiting, plaice, cod, haddock and mackerel, as well as smaller amounts of black sole, turbot, brill, John Dory and sea bream, which were prime fish at the time, as well as good quality prawns.

Usually, about twenty buyers took part in the auction, with few women among them. Most of the buyers strolled in well in advance of the sale to examine what was on offer and chat among themselves, although there were others who headed first to the nearby Roundy House, which was known as an early morning pub, as it opened its doors before normal business hours. If Mam was interested in a box of fish, she inspected it carefully, right down to the bottom. She checked the size of the fish underneath, as sometimes the bigger fish were deliberately placed on top and the smaller ones below. When the auction began, Jack Shanahan the auctioneer moved along from one box to the next. More often than not, about three buyers bid on each box.

Because the number of traders was quite small and also, I suppose, because they were in such direct competition – buying for the most part at the same auctions and selling from the same market – rivalries could become very intense. Also, the business was male-dominated. Two traders in particular went out of their way to make life difficult for Mam. I remember one making every effort to intimidate her, from small things like staying in the office in Clayton Love's while she was paying her bill, to real nasty behaviour, such as throwing a dead mouse in her stall when she wasn't around. But of course he only succeeded in making her more determined to make a go of it, and for every clown there tends to be several good people, and so it was in the market.

But she was lucky to have had that get-up-and-go attitude, as only the strongest survived. The market for fish was limited. Competition was rife. Everyone had to fight their own corner. And the fact that all the fish traders' stalls were located in the same area, away from the butchers and other English Market stall holders, made the rivalry even more intense, as the same produce was being sold on all sides.

All day, every day, the fishmongers watched each other's every move. They compared the number of customers at each stall and noted the people coming and going. They eyed up the range of fish on sale, the rate at which they were selling and the amount left over at the end of each day. They tried to eavesdrop on each other's conversations, too, to pick up any news, such as talk of a scarcity due in a certain type of fish, or the price paid for fish at the auctions.

For me, the auctions were a nightmare, especially on a cold morning, as Mam and I could be hanging around there for hours. And I was always anxious about the time, because I didn't want to be late for school. After buying the fish, Mam and I loaded the boxes on to a long, narrow trolley belonging to Clayton Love, with two big wheels in the middle and two smaller ones at the sides. Then we pushed the trolley together down the Grand Parade, across the road and into the market. Keeping the boxes in place wasn't easy, as we usually had about six in all, three below and three above. Often, when we tried to mount a kerb, we got stuck and had to hack back and try again.

Once we had unloaded the trolley, Mam walked me to school. Most mornings, I dreaded going in as I knew that the nun who taught me would slap me with a leather strap if I was late. She never showed me any mercy, even though she would have known that I'd been helping Mam. Apart from that, I loved school and have happy memories of being there. Every day, all the pupils got free fruit buns coated in sugar and bottles of milk, which were warmed by the open, classroom fire if the day was cold. My First Holy Communion day stands out in my mind. All the boys wore suits with a sash and paraded around the garden behind the school for photographs. Then, we all went inside with our families for tea and cakes.

Later, when I moved to Chríost Rí primary school on Evergreen Road, I settled in straight away. My best buddy Teddy Neville was there too. He lived only a few doors above my grandmother and we always hung around together, kicking a football out the back or chatting about our sporting heroes, among them the great hurler Paddy Barry, whom I often saw in action, as Dad was big into sport and took me along to the matches. Dad was a huge supporter of Saint Finbarr's GAA club, which is the only club in Ireland to have won All-Ireland club championships in both hurling and football. Often, he boasted that the team had the best crop of players in the land and sang the praises of Gerald McCarthy, Denis Murphy, Jimmy Barry-Murphy and Charlie McCarthy.

The Quiet One

Some days after school, I went back to the market and helped Mam behind the counter by wrapping fish for the customers in sheets of newspaper. Often she sent me off to O'Sulllivan's near the Mercy Hospital for bags of ice, which she used to preserve the fish in boxes overnight. The ice came in huge blocks, four feet by two feet by two feet, and the slabs were then crushed and divided into bags. I wheeled the bags on a hand truck – which was a small trolley with a ledge at the end – up through Castle Street and down onto the Grand Parade, then across to the market. When I got older, I put one bag across the handlebars and cross-bar of my bike and cycled back. Other times, Mam sent me for ice to Denis Burns' on Douglas Street. He exported a lot of fish, mainly periwinkles and wild salmon.

Often, I went to the *Cork Examiner* office on Academy Street for a few bundles of returned newspapers to use for wrapping fish. Sometimes, I did deliveries around the city, to houses and restaurants, on foot, or by bike with the deliveries on the carrier. Usually, I was lucky enough, but Mam got the fright of her life one day when she called to a house in Blackrock. A big, boxer dog appeared in the driveway. The owner said to Mam, 'He won't touch you.' But then, all of a sudden the dog jumped up on Mam and caught her clothes. After that, she was terrified and relied on me to do a lot of the deliveries.

But I wasn't the only one who helped Mam run the stall. Her lifelong friend Ettie Holland served behind the counter every Friday, as that was the busiest day. Ettie used to laugh aloud and say to Mam, 'Kay, you were made for this. Look at you, you've the gift of the gab and can serve the customers three at a time, no bother.' And she was right because Mam had a great way about her. She was chatty and customer-focused. Bit by bit, she built up her clients and they stayed loyal to her. Day in and day out, she strived to give them only the best.

As well as getting fish at the auctions, she also bought supplies from John Wright in Dublin, which arrived by train. She bought plaice imported by boat from Holland, as well as smoked fish from Mr Donnery at Foreman's on the Coal Quay, which he imported from Allan and Dey in Aberdeen, a highly respected fish processing company set up in 1890. If anything, Mam tended to be over-stocked rather than under-stocked, but that pushed her all the more.

After only a few years, Mam found herself on par with the rest of the established fish traders. But that wasn't good enough for Mam. She was ambitious and wanted to get ahead, to make her mark. She decided that the only way to do that was to have a bigger variety of fish on offer than any of her fellow traders. To get the extra supplies, she would need the right transport.

Years before, Dad had owned a scooter. Then he changed to a bubble car, which looked funny, not only because of its shape but also because it had two wheels in front and only one behind, and its only door was above the front wheel, which meant you literally got in by squeezing past the steering wheel. One evening, when we were driving home from a trip to Crosshaven, the car broke down. Two cyclists were passing by and one said to the other, 'Oh look, somebody has stuck a pin in their bubble.' Mam became highly indignant and made Dad get rid of the bubble car soon after. He replaced it with a Ford Anglia. Then he and his buddy Tim Lehane from Cobh made a trailer for the back. Now Mam was all set up to put her new plan into action, which was to head off on a two-and-a-half-hour journey to Castletownbere in West Cork and stock up on extra fish supplies not available in the city.

Dad drove and I went along too. Paul was too young and stayed behind with Pauline Browne, Mam's friend, who lived on Congress Road. Once we had made the first trip, Mam made up her mind that we should continue to go on a regular basis.

Usually we went twice a week, every Tuesday and Thursday. We'd set off about 5.00 p.m. Sometimes, I did my homework in the back seat. I never missed the journey, as Mam chatted all the way, giving a run-down on her day. Dad had plenty to say, too, as he was opinionated, just like Mam. Every now and then, Mam passed around a bag of sweets, as she never set out for an auction without stuffing her pockets with bags of Scots Clan, bulls' eyes and clove rock. If we touched down in Castletownbere in good time for the auction, which started at 8.00 p.m., we headed to Murphy's restaurant in the town for a bite to eat. Otherwise, we made do with snacks from home.

The auction was held indoors, in a hall on the pier. Usually, the fish from each trawler was weighed on its own and placed on a line on the floor. This meant that each bidder had to keep an eye on the position of the different types of fish and know the various amounts of each pile. Also, it was important to realise that it was pointless bidding big money on a certain type of fish early in the night, especially as a trawler down the line might have a surplus of that fish and sell it at a much cheaper price later in the night. Normally, when the auction began, about two thousand timber boxes of fish lined the floor, stacked one on top of the other, while trawlers continued to sail into the quay with more supplies on board. In comparison to the Cork auctions, there was more banter in Castletownbere and less tension, maybe because the buyers were not all from the same area but came from all over, with many from Cork, Killarney, Kenmare, Dublin and Limerick. As well as that, there were plenty of supplies to go around.

One night, only one trawler had a supply of prawns, about fifty boxes in total. In Castletownbere, if there were fifty boxes in one lot, anyone could bid. The highest bidder got the option of taking the lot or less, whatever number of boxes the bidder wanted, even if it was only one box. Then, the bidding started all over again for any left-over boxes. On that particular night, the two remaining bidders were a small street-trader from Killarney who wanted only one box and a Dutchman who bought for the export market. Neither would give way to the other and the prawns hit a high price, with the Dutchman being the last man standing. After the auction, he approached the man from Killarney and asked him if he needed a box of prawns, to which the Killarney guy replied, 'At that price, you must be joking!'

On the whole, the atmosphere was pleasant, although some nights it nearly came to blows. But Mam was smart enough to steer clear of trouble and always watched her tongue. One night, as she was chatting to three other buyers, a fisherman walked in with his catch. One of the men said, 'I wouldn't buy from him at all.' Then, the man beside him said, 'That's my brother you're talking about.'

Danny McCarthy from Kenmare, the owner of Star Sea-foods, had an eye for a bargain and Mam learned a lot from him. Danny always kept his eye on the ball, whereas some buyers often got distracted with talk and missed out on a good deal. Donal Connick, the auctioneer, helped Mam a lot too, and tipped her off if a scarcity was expected in a certain type of fish.

Mostly, the bidding was done with a nod and a wink. Usually, Mam bought about fourteen boxes each night. Sometimes, she got carried away and ended up with too much. When that happened, Dad would scratch his head and say, 'How in the name of heavens will I fit them all in?' But, there was always plenty of help on hand to load the trailer, as we had a great relationship with everyone there.

No matter what hour of the night we finished, Mam would always say, 'We'll go for a bag of chips so.' Dad and I would plead with her to sit into the car and go straight home. But she always got her way and the three of us would head off to the chipper in the town. Usually, I slept on the journey home. Mam and Dad sang all the way back, with Dad always making sure to sing his favourite song, 'I'll Take You Home Again Kathleen.' We rarely saw our beds before 1.00 a.m.

Yet the trip was well worth the trouble, as Mam quickly got the edge on the other fishmongers in the market. Often, I heard her say, 'Castletownbere made us. Have no doubt about that.'

Sometimes, instead of heading to Castletownbere for fish, we drove to the auction in Dunmore East, especially if the weather was bad, as conditions generally were not as severe in the south east as in the west. But Dunmore East was often wearing, as the auction didn't start until 9.00 p.m. and we had to wait until the entire sale was over before loading, which was not the case in Castletownbere.

Through all her years as a fishmonger, Mam used her common sense and thought things out for herself. In 1966, when Pope Paul VI ruled that abstaining from meat on a Friday could be replaced with another penance, the fishmongers went into a panic, all except Mam. She said, 'Look, not everyone sees fish as a penance food. People are paying good money to eat fish in restaurants. People do like it. And once the penance tag is taken away, maybe people will like it all the more.' At the start, fishmongers in the English Market did see a drop in fish sales. But, little by little, sales went up with many Catholics keeping the tradition, while others turned to fish as if it was something new and wonderful now that it had lost its penance tag.

Even though Mam always worked hard and never closed the stall until 6.00 p.m., except on a Wednesday, when she closed for a half day, she looked after us well. Every evening, she came home with our dinner, having cooked it in her small, two-ring stove in the stall. But, making sure we were well nourished wasn't the only thing on her mind.

One day, she got it into her head that I should take piano lessons, maybe because she thought I should follow in the footsteps of her brother Pierce, who was a gifted piano player. So, she packed me off to the School of Music, to a tutor called Jack Murphy, who had been a neighbour of hers when she lived in Mary Street. I hated those lessons with a vengeance. But that made no difference to Mam. She kept me at it. One morning, she went off to an auction at Marshall's in the city and bought a black piano, which she installed in the front room. Any time I sat down to practise, Dad came in to listen, to make sure that I was doing it right and not taking any shortcuts. I grew to detest that piano more and more each day and loathed any mention of Mozart or Handel. Mam and I had massive arguments and I made up every excuse under the sun to avoid going to the lessons or putting in some practice. All I wanted to do was play football. But she wouldn't give in and made me stick at it for eight, long dreary years. She sent Paul along for lessons too. He hated them every bit as much as me.

All through our childhood, Paul and I had been great buddies, even though there was a five-year gap between us. In many ways, we were like chalk and cheese, as he was chatty and outgoing, just like Mam, whereas I was the quiet one. At school, he was mischievous, partly because he was bored, while I was always studious.

By the time I went to secondary school, I'd had my fill of the fish stall and the English Market. It was the last place on earth I wanted to be. All my childhood had revolved around it and now I resented spending time there. I wanted to be like my pals, free to hang around together after school and play football. In my heart, I felt that Paul was the one most likely to eventually join Mam full-time in the market, not me. And Mam felt the same. At the back of my mind, I thought I might become a teacher. Yet life doesn't always turn out as expected and can often take us by surprise.

2

A Change of Heart

When I started secondary school at Coláiste Chríost Rí, I took to it like a duck to water. Founded by the Presentation brothers, Chríost Rí was a progressive boys' school, under the principal Brother Pious, with state of the art facilities, including a handball alley and a football pitch at the back. Well known for its teaching of Irish and its football, the school had strong links with the local Nemo Rangers GAA club, which always had a good representation on the Cork teams.

Through primary and secondary school, like all pupils I suppose, I've had good and bad teachers. Being honest, at Coláiste Chríost Rí I found most of them to be exceptional in both their ability and dedication, people like Brother Pious, Brother Colmcille, Martin Fahy, Bernard Martin, Kevin Cummins and Patrick Scanlon, who spent hours each day training teams on the pitch after school. The amount of time these people spent even outside of school hours helping pupils with both their studies and sport was immense. In latter years, when I read of the abuse perpetuated by some in positions of authority in our schools, I, like everyone else, was disgusted and horrified that people's lives have been ruined by the abuse they have suffered at the hands of these monsters. Yet I feel much sorrow too for the innocent members of religious orders whose great contribution to education and care was quickly disregarded, as it seemed that they became tarnished with the same brush and, as a result, lost people's respect.

Apart from maths, I loved all the other subjects, especially history and geography. In my class, I had loads of pals, among them Teddy Neville, John Janacek, Pat McCarthy, Eamonn Hurley, Declan Donnelly, Seán O'Flynn, Diarmuid Collins and Seán Martin, who later became the lord mayor of Cork and is a brother of the Fianna Fáil leader Mícheál Martin. Like all of my buddies, I was stone mad on hurling and football. Once I got a try for the school team as a goalkeeper, but Seán Martin beat me to it. The lot of us played in street leagues and with Nemo Rangers, where we mixed with our sporting heroes, men like Billy Morgan, the Cogan brothers and Dinny Allen. We were in awe of them all and loved the club with a passion, as everyone there always treated us well. Luckily for me, most of my matches took place on a Saturday, which meant I was able to go along, as the fish stall was closed.

Every weekday, I went to my grandparents' house for my lunch. Usually, Pop was the only one there. One day, not long after starting secondary school, I got no answer when I called. I ran up to Nan's shop in Barrack Street to tell Nan and Rosie. Nan said, 'Sure he must be there.' Rosie came back with me to the house. We found Pop sprawled over the kitchen table, after getting a heart attack. When I went to see him the following day in the South Infirmary, I got the fright of my life, as he looked so bad that I thought he was dead. Sadly, a year later, he died. He was waked at home in his bedroom, laid out in a brown habit. Against my will, I went up to say goodbye, which was a bad idea, because I had nightmares about him for months afterwards. I was broken-hearted without him, as we'd always been close, the best of buddies.

After Pop passed away, Mam came home a few days a week to give me my dinner. On those days, I cycled home at lunch hour with my pals Deckie Donnelly and Eamon Hurley. On busy market days, such as Thursdays and Fridays, I stayed in school at lunch time and went to the English Market after school.

Usually, Paul would be there too. By then, Mam had regular help. Every Thursday and Friday, a girl named Gretta Coleman – whom Mam said could talk for Ireland and was a great worker – served with Mam behind the counter, as well as Dad's sister Noreen.

Paul and I entertained ourselves by cycling around the city, or playing football in the alley leading on to Oliver Plunkett Street with our friend Kevin, who lived in an apartment nearby. Sometimes, if Paul and I were really good, Mam treated us to hot milk and cake in D'Arcy's café, which was popular with most of the market traders, among them Eileen Ahern, who ran a vegetable stall, and Mrs McDonald, who had a fruit and vegetable stall. Both of them were great friends with Mam.

In the market, Paul and I got to know not only Mam's best pals, but all the other traders too, such as Bert Bagnall, who ran a vegetable and fruit stall and advertised himself as Cork's most popular fruiterer, with satisfaction guaranteed. Bert bought in bulk and always gave his customers a good bargain. Mam was always over and back to him, as a big Avery scales for all the market traders stood right beside his stall. Babe Ann Kane sold offal, such as crubeens and pig's head, and arranged bus trips to Crosshaven every weekend. Paul and I were terrified of Mrs O'Sullivan, who ran a stall beside the fountain, as she was very exact and took no nonsense from anyone. At Christmas time, herself and Mrs Moynihan would have turkeys hanging from every nook and cranny of their stalls, so much so that if you stood there long enough they would probably hang one off you as well. The arrival of the turkeys created a great buzz, with customers hustling and bustling, eager to put in their order or haggling for a better price. Usually, they paid their bill over a few weeks, which meant extra work for Mrs O'Sullivan, as she had to keep track of each payment and enter it into her record book. Don O'Hare, who had a butcher's stall on the Princes Street end, was very grand in his ways and Paul and I would imitate his posh accent and laugh our heads off every time. Billie Mulcahy ran a fish stall. Before setting up on his own, he worked for another fishmonger, Ellen Corbett. When she passed on the stall to Billy and his co-worker, Billy bought out the other guy and became the sole owner.

Many of the stall holders employed messenger boys, who made deliveries on bicycles with big baskets on the handlebars and the name of the stall holders, their address and produce printed under the cross-bar. Many of the messenger boys lived on the north side of the city and cycled home for lunch every day. On their return, they often raced in groups back to the market, whistling and singing, pedalling at their hardest and swerving in and out between each other, trying to get ahead. When one such race got out-of-hand, somebody complained to the gardaí. Duly, the gardaí called into Mr Sheehan at his stall in the market to tell him to sort out the matter, as his messenger boy had been one of the main culprits. 'How do you know it was my fella?' asked Mr Sheehan, to which the garda replied, 'Because your name was on the bike.' Straightening himself up, Mr Sheehan answered, 'No problem. I will deal with that immediately.' When the bike arrived in the next morning, the name had been removed from it!

Usually, the messenger boys left the delivery bikes in the market overnight. But sometimes, if deliveries ran late, they took the bicycles home and neighbouring children queued up excitedly to cycle them.

Of all the messenger boys, Georgie Bear was the one Paul and I liked the best. His real name was George Martin, but he was nicknamed Georgie Bear, as he could carry a massive side of beef on his shoulders without any strain, even though he was tiny. On Wednesday afternoons, many of the messenger boys went to the cinema. Whenever a screen character was killed, the messenger boys shouted up, 'Georgie! Remove the body!' One night, I spotted Georgie staggering along on the Grand Parade, eating a bag of chips and the worse for wear after a few pints. He fell over, landed on the pavement and sat there, happily eating his chips, as if nothing had happened.

One day, when I was in my early teens, Mam asked me to pop over to Denis Burns on Douglas Street for ice. When I walked in, Jack Shanahan the office manager was chatting to Billy Mulcahy. He said, 'Jasus Billy, I hear you're after moving to a bigger fish stall in the market. You must be doing mighty well.' Billy smiled, gave me a quick glance and said to Jack, 'I tell you now Jack, I'll have the rest of them selling bleedin' vegetables.' Once I picked up the ice, I ran back to the market in a panic and told Mam what Billy had said. She laughed her head off.

Since the early 1970s, Garryvoe in east Cork became a major part of our lives. I suppose when you come from a family business, that business generally seeps into much of your life and most of the hours in your week. I believe, as my parents obviously did, that a pressure valve of some sort in your life is important. For us, Garryvoe was and still is that valve.

Although Garryvoe is only a thirty-minute drive from Cork city, in many ways it seemed like a million miles away, as being there was so different from life in the city. Originally, Mam and Dad had a caravan in Tramore in County Waterford. But they found it was too far away for weekend trips and also a bit too busy. In the early 1970s, they moved their 14-foot caravan to Ardnahinch in Garryvoe and so began a love affair for all of us with that east Cork resort.

During the summer months, we spent every weekend there, as Mam adored Garryvoe and loved the fact that it took less than an hour to get there from home. It became her haven, her special place, where she relaxed and switched off totally from the market. Dad and herself made loads of friends there, among them the owner of our caravan park, Wally O'Brien. They mingled with all their pals in Motherway's pub, where they listened to the music together, or in the local hotel, or in the nearby villages of Shanagarry and Ladysbridge.

Sometimes, they all gathered beside the caravans and chatted the night away, lazing back in their deck-chairs. Other nights, they started up a lively sing-song and sang their hearts out for hours on end.

Apart from having to be back at the caravan early every night, Paul and I had a ball, cycling around as free as the wind and playing football with all the other boys in our caravan park, which had about sixty caravans. Sometimes, we played matches against boys from the other two caravan sites. The rivalry was fierce and Paul and I gave it our all, as we were highly competitive. Most days, we picked periwinkles and spent hours in the sea, swimming and jumping with the waves. Sometimes, our friends Denis Ryan and Kevin Moynihan from Cobh took us fishing in their boat. Other days, we fished off the breakwater in Ballycotton, or we played pitch and putt there. We hung around the hall in Garryvoe too, trying our luck on the gaming machines, playing table tennis, or popping in and out to the disco at night. We were carefree and happy and relished the freedom. Then, when summer ended, we settled back into our old routine of going to school and the market.

As time drew nearer for me to sit my Leaving Certificate, I spent less time at the market and concentrated more on my studies. All the hard work paid off and I began a course at the Cork Regional Technical College in Business Studies, which was recommended to me by Pat Kelleher, the head of the department, who happened to be a customer of Mam's. The college was new and vibrant, having opened only about two years before I started there, with great lecturers, such as Tony O'Mahony and Damian Courtney. It was out to prove its worth, especially as its main competitor was University College Cork, which had been drawing the cream of students for decades. I soaked up all the lectures on marketing, communications and public relations but skipped those on accounting and economics. Instead, I played football or headed off for a game of pool or table tennis. But my bad habits caught up with me and I failed my first-year exams.

Yet playing sports wasn't my only distraction. In Garryvoe, I met my wife-to- be, Margaret O'Brien, although initially it was her younger sister Lillian who took my fancy.

Being the protective type, Mam and Dad believed that girls should not be on my agenda while I was still only about eighteen. When I look back, the innocence of those days still amuses me. Because of Mam and Dad's objections, my relationship with Margaret was fraught with arguments between myself and my parents, with neither side willing to give in.

Back in the city, Margaret and I kept the flame burning. As she lived nearby in Blackrock, we met often and usually zoomed around the city on my Honda 50, which Dad had got for me. Once, in the early days, when I visited Margaret at her home, I got locked into the bathroom, which had a dodgy lock. After trying for ages to get out, I heard Margaret's father in the hallway saying, 'Are you alright in there Pat?' Then, her mother Betty got into a fuss and said to him, 'Gerald, whatever you do, don't break the lock.' I had to climb out the window. Unfortunately, the door had to be opened and the only way to do it was to break the lock. That was certainly one of my more embarrassing moments.

It was not until my twenty-first birthday that Mam and Dad mellowed and warmed to my relationship with Margaret. In all my life, fighting for Margaret has been one of the hardest things I've ever done and she has been worth every single battle. Through thick and thin, she has been the rock in my life and the one who always puts emotion to one side and gives me the most solid advice.

In 1978, after graduating from college, I began work in the city with a brewery. But I stayed there only a day, as Dad got a temporary job for me with Cork Corporation in City Hall, as a supervisor of unemployed men, all of whom were older than me. It was a baptism of fire, but I can be a fast learner. The contract lasted about eight months.

After that, I stayed on with Cork Corporation and began work as an official in the rents department, which had about sixteen in the office at the time. Most mornings, I went out and about, on all sides of the city, collecting rent. On the whole, I never had any trouble, as most people paid on the spot. The wisecracks were mighty. One morning, when I knocked on a door on the north side of the city, I said to the man who answered, 'I'm looking for the rent.' He replied, 'Come in and we'll look for it together.' Another morning, in Mayfield, the home turf of Roy Keane, a nine-year-old girl came to the door. On seeing me, she shouted in to her mother, 'Mam, the rent man is here.' Her mother shouted back, 'Tell him I'm not here.' I loved their humour.

In the afternoons, I spent my time back at the office balancing books and lodging money in the bank. Often, I found it hard to balance the books and spent hours trying to get it right.

After about twelve months, I became bored with the work. Everyone else seemed happy enough with the job and appreciated its security. But I tired of it, as I found the work repetitive and often boring. Usually, being promoted meant a move to a desk job but working in an office all day long just was not on my horizon. If I worked any harder than anyone else, I felt I would only be showing up the others. It just wasn't for me. And although I enjoyed meeting people while collecting rent, and people were usually pleasant, I often felt like an unwelcome caller.

Deep down, I missed the market, even though it was a cold, draughty place to work, with constant pressure and competition, long hours and lots of manual labour. But I missed the buzz, the atmosphere, the sense of culture, the craic and the banter over the counter. The market had grown on me. Having moved away from it, I appreciated it all the more. And being aware that Mam had put so much effort into it, day in and day out for years on end, I felt a sense of obligation. And I think Mam always believed I would go back. Yet I knew it wouldn't be easy. I'd be the new kid on the block, as Mam now had three full-time workers, among them Paul, who had started there five years before, having left school early, and June Heaphy. June's sister Maura and her husband Kevin Murphy were life-long friends of Mam and Dad. By then, Dad had become more involved in the stall too and often helped out with filleting, collecting fish or making deliveries. Often at home, in recent years, when Mam, Dad and Paul discussed the stall, I felt left out, as I wouldn't have been in the thick of things. Now all of that was about to change.

And so, after working for two years with Cork Corporation, I said goodbye to my colleagues at City Hall and headed back to where I felt I belonged, in the fish stall at the English Market, a market with a history like no other.

3

The English Market

L ong ago, a market was defined as a meeting for buying or selling, or an open space or large building in which cattle, provisions or other commodities were offered for sale.

Down through the centuries, according to historical and archaeological proof, Cork city boasted many markets. Even prior to the establishment of Ireland's first towns by the Vikings and the use of money, Cork people ran a market at its most fundamental level by exchanging goods and labour in populated areas. During medieval times, the city depended on rural areas for much of its needs. Such trade was operated in a casual way, without regulation.

During the ninth and tenth centuries, the Vikings set up trading points at various ports, including one at the port of Cork. As the population of Cork grew, the city increased trade with its neighbours. After the Vikings introduced money to Ireland, it became more commonly used in the exchange of goods, especially in urban areas.

In the thirteenth century, Cork's internal and external trade increased, mainly due to a rise in population, an improvement in farming and a surplus of supplies. To generate money for themselves and to encourage trade in their boroughs, the

Anglo-Norman lords obtained a royal licence to set up annual fairs or weekly markets. As a result, a series of royal charters, beginning with that of Henry III in 1242, gave the successive corporations of Cork the exclusive right to run markets in the city. In 1299, the sheriff of Cork recorded thirty-six markets and market towns, many in the north and east of the area now known as County Cork. On a map drawn in 1545, Cork's market place is shown as an open space inside the walls of the city, north of the intersection of the city's two central islands, close to an area known today as Liberty Street.

Despite the rise of shops in Cork city, markets continued to thrive. By the late seventeenth century, markets were seen as a vital source of income for the corporation, which built, maintained and ruled them. Many markets began to specialise, particularly in the provision of meat, fish and corn. So too, trades became more proficient. Various guilds were formed, including guilds for bakers, goldsmiths, carpenters and butchers.

Until the seventeenth century, butchers often slaughtered animals in the street or the open market and then sold the meat there. In the seventeenth and eighteenth centuries, to put an end to the practice of killing animals and selling their meat on the street, meat markets were built. These purpose-built markets were known as shambles, or flesh shambles, as a shamble meant a bench and the word was associated with the butchers' benches or work blocks.

Built in the early 1690s, the shambles on Castle Street became the main meat market in the city centre and continued to trade until the Grand Parade Market opened in 1788. Located near Barrack Street, the South Shambles sold both meat and milk. Situated on the other side of the city, in the Shandon area, the North Shambles operated in an open space with a four-sided building in the middle. By the late eighteenth century, a triangle of buildings had been added to the site.

On maps from 1750, a narrow lane west of North Main Street is named as Fishamble Lane, which suggests that a fish shambles or market may have operated there. In 1758, a new fish market was built near Hanover Street. During the eighteenth century also, at least four milk markets operated in the city, including one built in 1747 at Old Market Place, off Blarney Lane. Potato markets too were popular, especially as the potato was the common food of the poor and was also enjoyed by the wealthy. Potatoes were sold not only in potato markets, but also in general markets, where a variety of foods were available. In particular, the sale of corn, such as oats wheat and barley, earned a considerable amount of income for the corporation. On maps of Cork dating from 1750, a rectangular building at the intersection of Cornmarket Street and Castle Street is named as Corn Market. The building also appears, unnamed, in an earlier map, drawn in 1726. In 1833, a new corn market was built on Anglesea Street. Other markets in the city included a herb market, a market selling butter and eggs, a fowl market, a fruit market, the Worstead Market, and the Frize and Bandle Cloth Markets. In 1769, the city's butter merchant traders set up the Cork Butter Market and it soon became the biggest butter market in the world.

From the outset, the corporation was committed to maintaining well-regulated markets, especially as the markets generated much income for the city authority by payment of rents for stalls or standings in the markets, and also by payment of tolls imposed on goods sold there. By 1780, to ensure cleanliness in the markets, the corporation collected annual deposits from stall holders. These deposits were held by the lord mayor and were used to pay cleaners to clean the markets if the stall holders failed to keep the markets at the required levels of hygiene. At the end of each year, the lord mayor returned the full deposit or any balance due to each stall holder.

In the 1780s, inspired by the contemporary covered markets in English cities, the Cork corporation, which was run by Protestants, decided to erect new, purpose-built, adjoining covered food markets in the heart of Cork city, between Princes Street, Saint Patrick's Street, Grand Parade and George's Street, which is now Oliver Plunkett Street. The site for the new market was surrounded by the comfortable homes and high-class businesses of Cork's wealthy merchants and elite, among them jewellers, perfumers and wine merchants. Clearly, then, the location of the new market suggests that it was meant to cater for the rich.

And so, the seeds were sown for the English Market, although the use of the name did not appear on any records until 1855, when it featured in a newspaper report. Seemingly, it was not its official name but rather a popular one, which may have come into use due to the fact that the market was run by a Protestant or English corporation, or to distinguish it from Saint Peter's Market, a second, central indoor food market, which was built on Cornmarket Street in the 1840s by a Catholic Irish corporation to cater for the working class and became known as the Irish Market.

In July 1788, several stalls in the Grand Parade section of the English Market were offered for weekly rent for one year, under the condition that only meat would be sold at each stall. On 1 August 1788, the new, unfinished stone-flagged market was officially opened. During the following year, fruit, fowl, fish and vegetable stalls were added. In 1789, the city's central fish market moved to a new site north of the Grand Parade meat market. The site was fitted with stone tables and had room for more than twenty stalls. Later, it became known as the Back Market, Little Market and Little English Market. In the early nineteenth century, the main market extended into the Back Market. Near Princes Street, a fowl market for the sale of poultry and a vegetable market were set up. In the 1790s, a narrow, roofless passage was created to link these markets to Princes Street. Similar to all the other markets in the city, the English Market was overseen by a Market Jury, which had the right to visit the markets and seize any unwholesome or illegally-held goods.

Mostly, supplies for the English Market came from market gardens in the city suburbs, particularly from those in Blackrock and Friar's Walk, as well as from farms in the surrounding areas. The market sold a wide range of vegetables and fruit, such as onions, cabbage, parsnips, turnip, carrots, celery, apples, strawberries, pears and plums. Butter and eggs were also sold, including buttered eggs, which had a rich taste. While beef and mutton were the most popular meats, other meats, such as poultry, pork, veal, lamb and offal were in much demand too. Spiced or salted tongue also sold well.

Although the fishmongers in the English Market offered a big selection of fish, bought from fish auctions in the city, fish was not as popular as meat. But sales of fish did increase in the nineteenth century due to the growth of Catholicism in the city, as Catholics obeyed the rules of abstaining from meat on holy days, Wednesdays, Fridays and during the forty days of Lent. However, such regulations may also have had a negative effect on fish sales, as linking penance to fish probably lessened its appeal. Rules regarding the storage of fish were strict and, in 1814, the lord mayor ordered that all fish brought to the city for sale should be delivered immediately to the market and not stored. Writing in the 1840s, Windele described the salmon from the River Lee as being much prized for its delicacy and superior flavour. In the mid-nineteenth century, due to the development of railways, the supplies and variety of fish increased greatly.

In the English Market, women traders were particularly dominant in the stalls selling eggs, butter, vegetables, tripe, drisheen and fowl. In 1856, one-third of the twelve fishmongers were women. In the nineteenth century, the number of female butchers in the market rose considerably. Some of the women were widows, daughters or other relatives of the butchers who had previously run the stalls. For various periods, between 1884 and 1893, thirty women had charge of stalls.

Over time, running family stalls and passing them on from one generation to another became a tradition, and vacant stalls were often taken over by young men and women who had served their time at the family stall. As a result, many of the stall holders were related to each other. Also, intermarriage between them was common.

In 1830, the corporation appointed an inspector, Robert Rogers, to manage the day-to-day running of the Grand Parade and Princes Street markets. His office was located in the market and his uniform consisted of a cap with a French peak, dark-blue, braided trousers, a frock coat and vest. The inspector had charge of two constables, or beadles, who policed the market, as well as two collectors and three weigh-masters, who later became known as scalesmen. The latter were responsible for the official weigh beam and scales, which were located at the centre of the market, and were paid a small fee by the butchers. The scalesmen weighed carcasses or large cuts of meat delivered to the market, as well as meat portions traded between butchers.

A post was also created in the market for an assistant, who sometimes took on the role of deputy inspector, and three sweepers were employed to keep flagged passages clean. The corporation also appointed a night watchman, with responsibility for lighting the market clock in winter and watching the butchers' goods. He was paid by the butchers. The busier butchers employed full-time messenger boys to deliver meat to customers either on foot or by bicycle, usually with a big basket in front. Others used the services of freelance messenger boys, who waited for work at the entrances to the market. After renovating the market in 1830, the corporation took over directly the collection of tolls on produce entering the English Market.

In 1835, a published parliamentary commission report on public corporations in Ireland implied that suppliers, traders and customers at the English Market were being exploited by corrupt officials for profit, particularly through the imposition of excessive tolls on goods coming into the market. In the elections of 1841, the Protestants were defeated by a Catholic majority and lost control of the corporation. Later, the new Catholic regime set up a Market Committee to oversee the administration of the markets.

Within the first two years of the Great Famine of 1845-1852, more than twenty thousand starving people had flocked to Cork city, where about five hundred people were dying every week. Beggars strolled through the streets and blocked the entrances to markets and shops. To avoid the disruption, many of the middle-class stayed away from the city centre. However, the English Market managed to keep trading during the famine years, with the market's beadles constantly on guard at the entrances to keep away vagabonds, and the lifestyle of the wealthy remaining relatively unaffected by the great hunger.

In the early 1850s, another commission report into the management and operation of markets and fairs in Ireland again identified the imposition of unjust tolls. At the time, the tolls charged in Cork were still based on a scale drawn up in 1711. Also, the report showed that the English Market earned Cork Corporation 18 per cent of its net income from all sources for the year ending 27 August 1851, while the combined revenue collected from all other nine city markets amounted to less than one-third of that from the English Market. These facts alone made the corporation realise the value of the English Market, as well as the importance of its upkeep and restoration, which they began to see as a worthwhile investment for the future. By 1855, the English Market boasted over seventy stalls in the main market and twenty in the Back Market, along with other stalls and open standings.

In 1862, the city engineer and famous architect Sir John Benson, with the assistance of a Mr Walker, drew up plans to renovate the Princes Street end of the market. Thomas Walsh acquired the building contract and work got underway to erect two houses with an ornamental front at the Princes Street entrance, to roof that entire section of the market and to build galleries there suitable for fruit and flower stalls.

On 19 December 1862, the newly-constructed market opened, to the delight especially of the female stall holders, who danced wildly around important corporation officials as an expression of their appreciation of their new stalls. The attractive front featured a twenty-foot high entrance, with a large arch made from black and white brick, as well as limestone mouldings. A big, semi-circular decorative light hung above the arch, with a round space overhead for a clock. Two beautiful new houses stood gracefully at either side of the entrance. These were especially designed as shops to generate rental income. Wooden beams and two rows of cast-iron pillars supported the angular, fluted glass roof, while the centre of the market allowed space for an ornamental fountain. The newly-revamped market was expected to be used occasionally for purposes other than the sale of produce, such as public meetings and exhibitions. However, such hopes failed to materialise until more than a century later.

Throughout the 1870s, other changes took place. Old, worn benches in the fish market, near George's Street, were replaced with marble counters, while new marble tables and water jets were also fitted. The wall at the back of the fish market was knocked and every second column was removed to create more space. The number of fish stalls increased and rent charges rose. Instead of being occupied by florists and fruit sellers as planned, the gallery had housed tripe and drisheen traders. These dealers were moved to the south-east end and the newly-available space for florists was advertised.

In comparison to the much-acclaimed new Princes Street entrance, the main access to the Grand Parade market looked dilapidated. In 1880, Terence O'Flynn secured the contract to build a new entrance and completed the work in July of that year. The centre of the new façade featured a clock supplied by Egan and Sons, with the Cork coat of arms positioned overhead and bearing the motto, 'A safe harbour for ships.' Over the northern gate, an inscribed slab showed the name of the market as the Grand Parade Market Buildings. The new entrance included four premises, which were advertised for letting to traders whose goods would not be in direct competition to those sold in the Grand Parade Market. However, the traders who leased the four stalls in the Grand Parade Market Buildings hit hard times, which led to rent reduction, rent arrears and a rapid turnover of tenants. A fall of business was also evident in the Grand Parade Market, with eleven stalls being idle there in 1889. Around this time, in an effort to attract trade and improve the appearance of the entrance, the restriction of forbidding the sale of meat in the four new shops was lifted.

In February 1887, the Tolls and Markets Committee re-roofed the Back Market, removed the stalls that separated it from the Princes Street Market and built newly-arranged stalls. However, by 1889, twelve of the twenty-nine stalls lay vacant and the Back Market continued to lose business. Over time, the Back Market closed down and was later leased to Lyons and Company, which had applied to use it as a warehouse. Meat stalls were built in the Princes Street Market and these helped to revitalise the area.

In the 1890s, further improvements took place within the market. Dogs were banned and the killing and cleaning of fowl there was prohibited. A better system of refuse removal was introduced, while additional stalls were connected to the main sewer and the whole market was painted. Also, the inspector became more thorough in detecting and removing bad meat, and old boxes used to display vegetables were replaced with wooden structures. Stalls were modernised and a new office was built in the gallery for the inspector.

Through the early twentieth century, improvements continued with the installation of new table tops, lights and sky-lights. Also, flooring and sheeting were laid and more stalls were connected to the main sewers. In certain cases, the corporation paid the full expense, while in others, such as in the building of offices in 1906, it shared the cost with the stall holders. After 1906, the burden of paying for most of the improvements fell to the traders themselves. The Public Health Committee and the Tolls and Markets Committee continued to enforce the various hygiene regulations. Refuse was collected twice each day, flagging in the fish market was altered to redirect the water to the back of the stalls, new toilets were installed, as well as a collective cooling chamber for meat, and the whole market was painted. In the 1930s, electric lighting replaced gas.

In the early twentieth century, the market began to show support for cultural nationalist ideas. In 1901, the corporation erected a flag in front of the Grand Parade Market, showing the Cork coat of arms, along with the Irish harp and shamrock. Also, tenancy agreements carried a new clause prohibiting the sale of foreign-fed beef, mutton and pork.

At that time, Ireland was still part of the United Kingdom. In 1912, in the interests of workers, the Liberal government introduced the Shops Act, which required traders to close for a half day each week. As a result, the fishmongers in the English Market agreed to close on Monday afternoons, while the rest of the stall holders opted to close at 1.00 p.m. each Wednesday.

During the First World War, food prices soared and trade declined, so much so that rent reductions were granted to traders in the English Market. In 1916, employees in the market played a prominent role in setting up the Cork Journeyman Butchers' Society, for which the market became a stronghold. By 1918, the Irish Trade Union Congress had already unionised many of the corporation's employees, including those working in the English Market. In particular, the trade union association supported the separatist nationalist movement that developed in the aftermath of the 1916 Rising.

After winning the general election of December 1918, Sinn Féin set up a secessionist parliament, Dáil Éireann, and declared an Irish independent republic. However, the Peace Treaty refused to recognise Irish independence and so, as a means of protest, on the day of the Peace Treaty celebrations, the English Market and all the other public buildings in Cork refused to close. In the local elections of January 1920, Sinn Féin proved triumphant yet again and won control of Cork Corporation. The commanding officer of the Cork IRA, Tomás MacCurtain, was elected as the city's lord mayor.

Under the new republican corporation, a Tolls and Markets Committee was appointed. The committee tried to carry on business as usual despite the horrific murder of Tomás Mac-Curtain by the Royal Irish Constabulary in March 1920, and the arrival of the Black and Tans and the Auxiliaries. Terence MacSwiney succeeded Tomás MacCurtain as both the lord mayor and the commanding officer of the IRA. In August, along with other IRA officers, he was arrested and jailed in Brixton prison, where he died on hunger strike in October, after fasting for seventy-four days.

In the wake of the Kilmichael ambush in November 1920, in which Tom Barry's flying column killed seventeen Auxiliaries, martial law was declared in Tipperary, Limerick and Cork. On the following night, the IRA murdered an Auxiliary and wounded twelve others at Dillon's Cross in Cork. Allegedly in retaliation, the Black and Tans and the Auxiliaries went on a burgling and burning rampage through Cork. They destroyed city hall, a library and most of Saint Patrick's Street, as well as some nearby streets. The roof of the Princes Street market was badly damaged and two stalls were burned as fire spread from a nearby department store. Stalls in Market Lane were also ruined.

After the War of Independence, the Republicans retained control of Cork until the end of the Civil War, when the city was taken by troops of the Free State. By then, the city was in a poor state due to the effects of four years of violence and the disruption of trade. An enquiry into the municipal affairs of Cork showed that the corporation – which had worked without a proper base since the burning of city hall – had been negligent in carrying out its duties. Also, the report stated that the English Market, which had been running at a loss in recent years, was overstaffed. To offset the losses, rents in the market were increased.

As a result of the findings of the enquiry, the city's council and its fifteen committees were dissolved, including the Tolls and Market Committee, and replaced by a city commissioner, Philip Monahan, who was known for his ruthlessness in tackling administrative affairs. Straight away, he sacked staff at the English Market, among them all the constables and scalesmen, and he imposed harsh wage cuts on those who remained. Over time, the market began to show profit. Vacant stalls were offered to the highest bidder, which resulted in a break in family continuity, a decline in the number of specialist butchers and an increase in general or mixed stalls, such as those selling vegetables, tripe and drisheen.

The English Market

In the late 1920s and 1930s, due to high unemployment and poverty in the city, the English Market began to cater more and more for the working class and changed its range of goods to suit its customers. In the early 1940s, at least twelve stalls lay idle. In 1955, the traders in the Irish Market received notice to vacate their stalls and were offered stalls in the English Market instead. By 1958, the English Market housed seventy-four traders, including thirty butchers and nine fishmongers. Each morning, it opened at 8.00 a.m. and closed at 6.00 p.m., except on Wednesdays when it closed for the afternoon and on Saturdays when it closed at 7.00 p.m. At the time, a report in the *Evening Echo* described the English Market as the barometer of the city, as the extent of its trade reflected the financial state of the city.

In 1962, due to intense pressure from the Department of Health, many improvements were carried out at the market, including the cementing of floors and the installation of a new drainage system. Also, the building was painted and each stall received its own water supply and sink. Until then, stall holders had washed their vegetables at the market's fountain. The new improvements revitalised the market. Furthermore, the arrival of a new, energetic, Cockney fruit trader, Bert Bagnall, drew many new customers into the market and increased its overall trade. In 1967, the market was further enhanced with the opening of the Market Parade, which gave additional access from Saint Patrick's Street through the old Back Market. In the 1970s, more refurbishments were carried out, with the erection of a new roof and the laying of new flooring. Also, stalls were improved and a new system was introduced whereby each stall holder would receive a lease for twenty-one years and a rent review every five years, with the annual rent being based on square footage. Service charges and rates also applied.

By 1979, when I started working full-time at the English Market, its future looked secure. But the reality would prove otherwise, as many trials and tribulations lay ahead.

4

Early Days

For me, returning to the English Market was very much a two-edged sword. On the one hand, I immediately felt at home there and was more content in myself and in what I was doing. On the other hand, things had moved on. It's strange, but when you work in a place like the market every day, you don't notice the subtle changes that go on all the time. Yet when you leave for a few years and return, you feel that everything has changed.

To begin with, Paul had left school early and was well established in the market with Mam. Both had their own particular tasks, habits and ways of doing things. Everyone else had their routine and systems in place and here was I parachuting in with a certificate in Business Studies under my belt and almost two years experience with Cork Corporation. Full of confidence, I thought that I knew it all and could change the world. But I soon learned that changing the world was not that easy. I realised that customers had their own favourite people behind the counter by whom they wanted to be served, and that I would have to knuckle down and build up my own customer base. It's strange but thirty years later I see my daughter Emma and my nephew Seán in exactly the same situation, thinking that, because their family run the stall, they can just come on board and have their own way. Business shouldn't and doesn't work like that. Everyone must start at the bottom and work their way up to earn any respect.

Most mornings, Paul, Mam and I opened the stall at 7.00 a.m. Then we unloaded the van, which more often than not was filled with fish we had bought at the Castletownbere auction the night before. We spent an hour or more setting up the counter. By then, our two co-workers would have joined us and the early-morning customers would have started to come. We worked a six-day week, as Mam decided to open on Saturdays and the half-day during the week had gone by the board.

Apart from serving customers and taking orders over the phone, I spent much of my day filleting and packing fish. In between, I constantly sharpened my knives on a stone block and then smoothed them off on a steel block. There was a knack in doing it and a bit of luck involved too. On Wednesdays and Fridays, I made deliveries in the van, mostly to restaurants in Kinsale. Some nights, I drove to Castletownbere for fish, either alone or with Paul or Mam. Occasionally, I headed to the auctions in Galway. Many mornings, Paul and I set out at 5.00 a.m. for Union Hall in West Cork to collect fish.

At all times, even when we were up the walls, we did our best for the customers, because in Mam's eyes the customers always came first. She made sure to have a laugh with them and the rest of us had to live up to her high standard of service. If there was a customer waiting to be served and we were due to take a lunch break, getting that break always took second place.

All in all, I settled in well at the fish stall and came to realise that the English Market was not only a place of business, but also a place of interaction, where traders listened to customers' good news and troubles, engaged in a bit of banter and took some slagging too. I quickly learned that nothing can ever be taken for granted where trade is concerned. This proved especially true one morning when we got totally unexpected bad news.

At about 5.00 a.m. on 20 June 1980, the whole house awoke to the sound of the phone ringing in the hall. Instinctively, we knew that getting a call at that hour of the morning meant bad news. To this day, I can't recall who was on the other end of the line. But the message was short and direct, 'The market is on fire.' Our initial reaction was that this was someone with a really nasty sense of humour. How could the market possibly be on fire? After all, it had stood there for hundreds of years. Of course, reality kicked in pretty quickly and we dressed as fast as we could and drove to the market without delay.

When we pulled up at the Grand Parade end, which is where we always enter the market, the building looked all right, although we knew by the sight of the many active gardaí and fire personnel that this was not the case. On approaching the market, we could see that the Princes Street end had been badly damaged. By then, the fire department had the blaze well under control. To our relief, we learned that the Grand Parade end had not been affected. At that stage, we were not allowed to enter the building.

Outside on the Grand Parade, the traders gathered in huddles. We heard that the fire had started at about 11.30 p.m.

and later learned that it was caused by a gas explosion. As the market had a timber structure, the fire spread quickly. At one point, the flames shot thirty feet high into the air and became visible from many parts of the city. The roof and gallery swiftly collapsed on to the stalls on the ground floor. Six units of the city's fire brigade fought the blaze and, to their eternal credit and professionalism, managed to contain the fire to the Princes Street end – no easy task, especially with all the surrounding old buildings and limited access.

Standing on the Grand Parade, the sense of loss was unbearable, especially as nobody knew what was going to happen in the short or long term. Would the Grand Parade side re-open immediately? Would the Princes Street end be re-built? And, if so, what form would it take? The choking stench of the smoke, the water hoses, the fire brigades, the guards, the gathering crowds, all filled us with a sense of total loss and devastation, so much so that when we were eventually allowed to enter the market some time later, there was almost, and I stress almost, a sense of relief that so much of the market had survived. My abiding memory of that morning was seeing the fountain on the Princes Street end still standing proud in the middle of total devastation and chaos, and thinking quietly to myself, headstone or phoenix?

In total, eleven stalls were put out of business that morning. And even though the corporation re-built the Princes Street market within eighteen months of the fire, some of the stall holders never returned. However, on that particular morning, the future looked very bleak indeed.

As it happened, the fountain proved to be a phoenix. The re-building of the market was estimated at €300,000, but the insurance covered only €150,000. Yet it quickly became evident that the corporation had no intention of losing any of this jewel in the middle of Cork city. One way or another, the balance would be found. City architects Jack Healy and Des Berkeley took on the task of planning the restoration under a tight budget and the renovation began in January 1981.

To remain true to the original form of the market, the craftsmen used any remaining important features as models and based improvements on the original architecture. They restored the fountain to its former glory and placed it in a prominent point, on the axis of the Princes Street exit, a little away from its former position. A Canadian painter touched up its ironwork and one of its birds received a new wing. The floor was laid in small ceramic tiles, while the curved form of the original roof was re-done in laminated timber which brought more daylight into the market. On the ground floor, eleven new stalls were built, with divisions of modern, concrete brick walls between each one. A new first floor gallery was also erected, with a café on the north side and five new stalls separated by brick walls. Traditional techniques were used to cast new iron brackets in a sand-bed template carved from surviving features. All brickwork and stonework, both indoor and outdoor, were cleaned, repaired and re-pointed.

With all the restoration complete, stalls in the Princes Street end of the market re-opened for business on 30 October 1981 to a flurry of excitement, with city shoppers eager to get a glimpse of the much talked-about revamp and see the new stalls for themselves. But not all of those affected by the fire returned, as some went into retirement, among them Don O'Hare, who ran who ran a very successful butcher stall, while the O'Flynns moved to Marlboro Street.

In 1983, the restoration project received a gold medal from Europa Nostra, the international federation of conservation societies, for its contribution to the enhancement of the architectural heritage of Europe. Jack Healy, Des Berkeley and O'Shea's builders should be justifiably proud of what they achieved.

While the award gave cause for celebration and brought great prestige to the English Market, the fire of 1980 left an indelible mark on all of the traders there, as it stood as a stark reminder to us all that our livelihoods could disappear in the blink of an eye.

As soon as Cork Corporation started re-building the Princes Street end of the market after the fire, everyone assumed that the market would be booming again. Nothing could have been further from the truth. The market was now starting to struggle and struggle badly. In particular, the fish aisle was in a sad state, with several units empty. Joe McHugh, the city manager – and one of the best we ever had – visited the market frequently. Constantly, Mam nagged him over the vacant units, as they ruined the overall appearance of the fish aisle and Mam wanted to have a full, active fish aisle in operation. Joe told her it was impossible to get tenants to take up units in the market at that time. Eventually, out of frustration, Mam asked Joe if she could open two of the units further down the aisle to use for filleting and preparing orders. At this stage, I think Joe must have been as frustrated as anybody at not being able to fill units and he readily agreed.

At the time, a butcher's fridge separated our original stall from the new units, which were situated in an awkward area, as a laneway ran through its centre. Cork Corporation had blocked off the outside of this lane and were using the space as an office for the market's cleaners. It was not an ideal situation, as the cleaners had to walk right through the centre of our new units to exit the office.

Soon after we started filleting in the new units, customers began to buy fish there. So Mam decided that Paul and herself would run the original stall and that I would take charge of the new units and sell fish there, instead of just filleting. Taking over those new units was the makings of me, as it gave me the chance and confidence to run a business.

Now we had two counters being operated by the same family within ten feet of each other. Customers looked on them as two totally separate businesses and many shopped only at one and never at the other, which always amused me.

Mam tiled her entire stall and did it up in the old-fashioned style, with a traditional, open-top flat counter. In contrast, I opted for a counter with a glass covering in front. I found it a nightmare to clean, as I had to lift up the glass and be extra careful not to let it slip. In practical terms, it was unsuitable for a fish stall, but it looked highly modern and hygienic. For the walls, I chose white tiles at the top and black at the bottom. Both units were now fully modern and well equipped with big fridges and refrigerated stainless steel counters, all a far cry from the original tarmacadam floor, marble-slab counter and walls covered in wallpaper.

Then, the rivalry set in. When we got word of a competition being run by the Cork Business Association for shop fronts, we entered both stalls, as we were hugely competitive. Funnily enough, we were awarded joint first.

Yet we were lucky to have modernised at that particular point, especially as we were now facing strong competition from new, well-positioned shopping centres. These began to pop up in many suburban areas of Cork, such as Douglas and Wilton. Suddenly, the food business became much more competitive.

By then, Clayton Love had closed down and we were buying the bulk of our fish from Castletownbere, with smaller amounts coming from Cobh, Galway, Dingle and Union Hall. On the whole, business looked set to improve, especially when we became regular suppliers to many restaurants, among them a newly-opened Chinese restaurant in Patrick Street, which bought much bream, squid, black sole and sea bass. The owners had a different tradition to the Irish and ordered the fish whole, not filleted. They knew their fish, bought in big supplies and paid cash on the spot. We supplied many other restaurants too, especially in Kinsale, which was building a reputation as a gourmet destination, with a mixture of talented local and foreign restaurant owners, such as Philip and Joss Horgan at Man Friday, Mrs McNiece at The Spinnaker Bar and Restaurant, Brian Cronin at The Blue Haven Hotel, Bobby and Maura Carpenter at The Overdraught, Michael Riese at The Vintage, as well as Tom Farrell at Robert's Cove Inn. These gifted, go-

*My Communion day in
the gardens of South
Presentation Convent, 1964*

*Me and Paul sitting by the front
door of our home in Friar's Walk
– the best of buds*

*Kathleen and her two boys –
happy days*

*Always laughing, Paul
and myself messing at
Garrettstown*

My Confirmation photo

Love the anorak – probably taken in Youghal, County Cork

With Mad and Dad checking out the fish stalls on Moore Street

*Kathleen obviously wasn't too impressed
with this fish display in Spain*

And showing a German visitor how it's done

Sorry mate, our display in Cork is so much better
– by the way, never turn your back on the customer

Paul's 21st in Ashburton House – what a night!

*Margaret with our
daughter Sarah*

*My cousin Imelda with her son
Sean – Imelda used to collect me
from junior school, lucky me*

My Aunt Noreen with her grandson, Dad and my Uncle Paul

*Mam with Dad's sister Rose – taken in Georgia, USA,
when Rose went to live with her daughter Imelda*

*Mam and Dad with Mam's favourite brother,
Dick, and his wife Mary*

Pop catching up with the news in Evergreen,
and having a cigarette and a drink with a friend

The women in my life

*Call of duty – incredible photo of a fireman
silhouetted by the flames against the night sky*

*Utter devastation – would the horrific 1980 fire in the English
Market represent a headstone or a phoenix for the market?*

ahead people put Kinsale on a world stage, with fish being a strong selling point on all their menus.

Also, through increased dining out, travelling further afield and the new phenomenon of the celebrity chef, fish was becoming more popular in Ireland. Instead of filming cookery programmes mainly in television studios, mobile film crews began to go out and about, all over Ireland, to meet and film those involved in the food industry. Naturally, the English Market became the ideal place for this new type of show. Through these programmes, presenters such as Keith Floyd, Derek Davis and Myrtle and Darina Allen all did great work in raising the profile of Irish food and Irish cooking. In particular, they placed a special emphasis on fish.

All of a sudden, people took notice of the great quality and huge choice of food available on our doorstep. A wonderful sense of adventure and confidence ensued. When shopping for food, people became choosy. They began to look for greater choice and demanded better quality. Of course, this suited the English Market to a tee. Over time, traditional fish, such as smoked cod, whiting, mackerel and haddock, were pushed aside in favour of bass, turbot, black sole, bream, hake, prawns and scallops. As the market is so sociable, people found it easy to make the transition there. If customers were unsure about a certain type of fish or how best to cook it, they could ask for advice and would leave the market very much at ease with their purchase, even if it was a fish they had never before tried. Even to this day, one of the market's best attractions is the fact that the traders still give their customers all the time they need to become confident and comfortable with their purchase. If they need help, all they have to do is ask.

One particular funny incident stands out in my mind about a customer who failed to ask for help before cooking fish with which she was totally unfamiliar. On a Thursday, the woman bought around £200 worth of lobster from me for a dinner party, which she intended hosting on the following Monday night for her parents and in-laws. On the Monday morning, she phoned me in a panic and told me that the lobsters had died, even though she had kept them in a bath of water all week-end, thinking that they would stay alive. I explained to her that of course they had died, as lobster must be cooked within a couple of hours of purchase or kept in a special sea water tank. Luckily, we had lobsters in our tank and we cooked them up for her, ready for collection that very evening. The dinner party went off without a hitch, with her in-laws convinced that their son had made a great match. Several years passed before she actually told them the full story.

Another lobster story comes to mind about a man who went into Martin Shanahan's shop in Kinsale and bought all the lobsters in Martin's fish tank. Then, he promptly released them all back into the sea, as an act of kindness. On returning to the shop the next day to tell Martin of his so-called good deed, he nearly had a seizure when he found that Martin had re-stocked his tank.

With fish becoming ever more popular, we needed extra storage space. At the time, we had an old garage, which Dad had made out of old Ford boxes from the local factory. I have fond memories of helping him by hammering in some nails as he painstakingly put it all together. That garage lasted twenty years, a testimony not only to Dad's skill but to the durability of the boxes as well. In those days, people were known to have built holiday homes in Crosshaven from these boxes. To create the extra storage space that we needed, Dad decided to knock the old garage and build a new block garage further down the back garden, with a cold room at the back in which we could store fish when we returned late at night from Castletownbere or Dunmore East. If we were under pressure in the stall, it also allowed us do a little filleting there at night. I have no recollection of ever seeing a planning notice, but times were different then. And, we had great neighbours, as nobody ever said a word.

About two years after I started full-time in the fish stall, Margaret and I married. Our wedding day took some unusual twists and turns and became one of the most unforgettable days of my life.

5

Wedding Bells

A week before my wedding on 30 May 1981, thieves broke into our house in Friar's Walk and ransacked the place, emptying drawers, overturning mattresses, pulling out cupboards, but miraculously not bothering with the wedding presents – or so we thought – which were stored in the front room.

On the morning of the wedding, I got up early, as I hadn't slept well anyway. To be sure to be sure, I decided to double-check everything for the big day. In only a matter of minutes, I found out that one of the thieves must have been a size ten in a shoe, as my wedding shoes, which had been left in the front room with the presents, had disappeared. Of course, I asked Mam if she had moved them, as Mam always had a habit of re-arranging things, but she said she never touched them. Paul and Dad hadn't shifted them either. But there was no need to panic, as I had plenty of time.

So I headed off into the Central Shoe Store on the Grand Parade. As the shop was still closed, I strolled in to the market to see how Noel was getting on. Noel was supposed to open our stall at 7.00 a.m. and the girls were due in about 10.00 a.m. There was no sign of Noel. Still, there was no need to panic, so I phoned Mam, told her that I'd open up the stall and asked her to send a taxi for Noel. At 10.00 a.m., there was still no trace of Noel and I still had no shoes. But, no panic, still a bit of time left. Once again, I rang Mam and asked her as politely as possible to fill me in on what was happening, although at this stage I felt like screaming, 'Where the hell is Noel?' With great calmness, she reassured me that Noel was on his way and that there was plenty of time.

Eventually, at 10.30 a.m., Noel arrived. I quickly told him that I had done some of the restaurant orders and that the rest were written in the order book, and I asked him if he missed the bit about me getting married that very morning at noon. Then I hurried out to the Central Shoe Store, bought the shoes, ran home, showered, dressed and headed off to Saint Michael's Church in Blackrock. No panic really.

Sitting on the right-hand side of the altar with my wife-to-be, best man and bridesmaids, my blood pressure was just beginning to return to normal when, out of the corner of my eye, I spotted a total stranger approaching the altar. At this stage, the wedding ceremony was well under way. Having calmly stepped over the altar rails, he walked up to me and asked, 'Where is the fish for Hunter's Lodge Restaurant?' Somewhat shocked, I said, 'Sorry?' Again, he asked, 'Where is the fish for Hunter's Lodge Restaurant? Noel can't find it.' My first thought was that my marriage would be over before it even started, but, minutes later, my stunning bride said, 'I do.' I guess she knew me better than I thought.

On our honeymoon, there was one more little surprise to come. When I opened my suitcase, which I had carefully packed, I found my mother had squeezed in seven pairs of new pyjamas. Margaret laughed for two full weeks.

As a family, we learn from our mistakes. So some years later, when Paul was making plans to marry, it was decided that Saint Patrick's Day would be an ideal day for the wedding, as the market would be closed.

For the past few years, we had supplied the crew of Brittany Ferries with smoked salmon when they docked at Ringaskiddy. Two days before Paul's wedding, a member of the crew rang to say that although she knew that Saint Patrick's Day was a public holiday, she would be very appreciative if we could deliver the salmon that day, as the ship's schedule was changed because of the holiday weekend and it would be docking early in the morning. As Paul's wedding was booked for 2.00 p.m., we decided to go ahead with the delivery.

On the morning of the wedding, Paul and I drove the twenty-minute journey to Ringaskiddy. As soon as the passengers disembarked, we climbed on board the ship and went straight to the reception as usual. We were totally calm, as we had plenty of time. The crew began to arrive for their smoked salmon and everything was going well. Then, the receptionist came over and told us that, because the ship was staying in port for the day, it would have to move over to the opposite berth, which should take about twenty minutes. She said that we could get off there, although it would take us slightly longer to walk back to our van. As the crew had more time than usual, we were selling a lot of smoked salmon. Paul and I looked at each other and decided to stay on board while the ship moved, as we had many hours yet before the wedding. No panic.

Almost immediately, the ship began to move. We kept on selling merrily away. After about ten minutes, the ship stopped. The crew began to disappear to their bunks as we gathered up the last few sides of smoked salmon and headed down the stairs to the car deck, where we usually disembark.

When we got to the car deck, we realised that the door was closed. That was unusual. And there was nobody around, which was also strange. Still, we kept calm. We headed back upstairs to the reception. The place was eerily quiet, with no sign of life. When I strolled over to the window and looked out, all I could see was water. Then, when I rushed over to the window at the opposite side, it was the same story – water, water everywhere. To my horror, I realised that the ship was stopped in the middle of the channel, not at the berth. Still, we had plenty of time, no panic. But by now I was getting a horrible sense of *déjà vu*. Eventually, we found one of the maintenance men who told us in broken English that the ship would not be docking until another ship had unloaded, which would probably take about three hours. At this point, Paul was seriously thinking of swimming ashore until I reminded him that he didn't know how to swim, although he must have been thinking it would be better to drown a hero rather than face the wrath of Marian and explain how he ended up being very, very late for their wedding. With great faith in the power of prayer, I began saying the quickest decade of the rosary since the one I said on the morning of my own wedding. When we spotted the Cobh pilot boat at the side of the ship, we raced down the stairs, just reached it before it pulled away from the ship and hitched a ride ashore.

When we ran in home, just in the nick of time to get ready, Mam appeared, all decked out in her wedding finery, and said, 'What the blazes kept ye?' Having spent two weeks writing my best man's speech, I promptly put it in the bin, as obviously the unexpected drama of the morning gave me just the ammunition I needed for a few laughs.

However, if Paul thought for one moment that he had seen the end of the wedding trauma, he was sadly mistaken. Before they got married, Paul and Marian had bought a house in Hollygarth in the city suburb of Douglas. The whole outside of the house was painted. Convinced that its upkeep would prove costly and time-consuming, Mam thought it would be a great idea to have it pebble-dashed while Paul and Marian were away. So, while the newly-weds were boarding the plane to set off on their honeymoon, Mam was moving the builders in to their house. When Paul and Marian returned two weeks later, they never recognised their own house and drove right on past it. Naturally, all hell broke loose, although the pebble dash is still there.

6

Changing Times

Although the restoration of the Princes Street end gave the English Market an initial boost to business, it was very short-lived, as the market, the city and the country tried to survive the horrible recession of the 1980s. Almost overnight, employment in Cork city got hammer blow after hammer blow, leaving not only the market but the whole city reeling.

In a short space of time, major companies such as Verolme Cork Dockyard, the Ford car factory and the Dunlop tyre factory, which were very much part of the Cork landscape, closed their doors. These well-paying companies had been the mainstay of Cork's economy and the foundation of its strong business. Many people in the city had believed that these firms were permanent fixtures and hundreds of other jobs sourced from these big companies had been dependent on their survival.

Once Michael Ryan of the Arbutus Lodge – one of the finest restaurants in the country at the time – showed me a blank cheque from Ford's. Some of its American executives had recently visited the Cork plant and dined at the Arbutus the previous evening. Such was the trust and relationship with the restaurant that, at the end of the evening, the cheque was signed, but otherwise left blank.

The closure of Ford's and other key companies ripped the heart out of the city and affected its entire business, cultural and social fabric. As a result, Cork seemed to lose its confident swagger and belief. Emigration became rife. Employment choices disappeared. Highly skilled workers, young graduates and young families left Cork in their droves and went abroad in search of employment and a better lifestyle.

In no time at all, the city found itself swimming against a very cruel tide of a failing local economy, high unemployment, social problems and local budgeting difficulties. Like the rest of the city, the English Market struggled badly. As well as trying to cope with tough competition from the ever-growing number of supermarkets, the market had to deal with other serious issues. The stall holders in the market were ageing, with little new blood coming in. All of a sudden, the number of units closing down became a huge concern. An air of doom and gloom hung in the air and the future looked bleak. Stall holders panicked and began to look at neighbouring stalls as their competitors, rather than at the more important competitors that the market was facing from outside. They started to cut prices. Quality suffered and the race to the bottom began. Up until then, the English Market's trump card had always been, and always will be, quality produce, local where at all possible, at a fair price.

Being stubborn, my mother refused to get drawn into this cycle. Instead, she stood steadfast to her belief that the market must cater for everybody, as this was one of the market's major attractions. With great determination, she insisted that we stayed true to our slogan, 'As fresh as it gets.'

To add to the struggles of the traders, on 6 January 1986, disaster struck again when fire ripped through the Princes Street end of the market for the second time in six years. The blaze began on the gallery, above Moynihan's stall, and burned four stalls there, along with another four on the ground floor. Some of the roof was also damaged. We were shocked that the market had caught fire for a second time, especially as we had been told that an alarm and sprinkler system had been installed. That annoyed us more than the actual fire, which was not as extensive as the first blaze. The eight traders affected were put out of business temporarily as repairs got underway, at a cost of about £150,000.

Only two years after the fire, the whole future of the market came under serious threat when Counsellor Seán Beausang presented a proposal from private developers to demolish the markets and replace them with a multi-storey car park and shopping centre, with ground floor space for a market area. Thankfully, the plan never saw the light of day.

While the early and mid-1980s were a time of huge concern for the traders of the English Market, and indeed for our landlord Cork Corporation also, the late 1980s and early 1990s began to give hope.

As with all gradual changes, it's hard to put a finger on exactly what triggered this revival, as several things happened over a period of time. Cork Corporation handed over the day-to-day running of the market to Irish Estates Limited, which specialised in retail property management. New stalls opened up and new blood arrived in the market in the form of Driss Belmajoub at Mr Bell's, Anne-Marie Jaumaud and Martin

Guillemot at Maughanaclea Farm Cheeses, Toby Simmonds at the Real Olive Company and Seán Calder-Potts at Iago. All of these additions of exotic and local foods, along with the traditional market foods, gave the market the traction it needed. In my mind, the icing on the cake was the arrival of Kay Harte and the Farmgate Café and Restaurant on the gallery, which had previously been an under-used and neglected space. Now, as well as being able to purchase raw materials downstairs in the market, customers could also taste the great variety and quality on the gallery. I always say that Kay Harte's restaurant must be one of the very few in Ireland that does not need to have a fridge as all her ingredients come from downstairs in the stalls. Other excellent restaurants in Cork also use produce from the market, including Nash 19, Jacques, Crawford Gallery, 14A, Les Gourmandises, Isaacs and Cornstore.

Now, with the market set to thrive, everyone wanted a piece of the action, especially the media. A new Irish food culture began. Famous food broadcasters and writers, such as Tom Doorley, Keith Floyd and Myrtle and Darina Allen, kept promoting Irish produce and the food at the English Market. Time and time again, the market featured in televised food and tourism shows, as well as on radio. Local and foreign newspapers and magazines hailed it as Cork city's main attraction and dubbed it as, 'The best of all worlds under the same roof.'

In the mid-1990s, the English Market became a popular night-time venue for cultural events, such as fashion shows, poetry readings, food fairs, song recitals, plays and art exhibitions. On these occasions, the market took on a festive air of celebration, a carnival atmosphere. Laughter and chatter echoed all around. Stalls stayed open for the duration of the events and traders had more time to talk with the customers, often to the background of lively, traditional music or jazz and flickering candles, casting dancing shadows on the walls and sweeping us back in time to another age.

Many nights, Paul or I drove to Castletownbere, Dunmore East, Kilmore Quay or Galway for fish. An odd time, the auctioneer there named Brian Casburn bought at the auctions for us. But that meant we had to pay a bit extra and maybe miss out on a bargain. Sometimes, we headed for Killybegs, to the auction hall on the pier, especially during bad winters when the fishermen there seemed to be the only ones catching fish. We became regular customers of Bob Thompson from Cobh, who was a great fisherman and who owned a boat called the *Mona Lisa*. Mostly, Bob supplied us with cod, plaice, hake and whiting. If the weather was good, we called down to him every night to collect supplies. The only drawback was that we had to buy whatever he happened to have, which was not always what we wanted and was not the best scenario for our type of business. But we had a great relationship with him and his wife Ada, as well as with their helper, a lad named Eric, who always went out fishing with Bob. Ada dealt with the weights and money. She haggled away with Mam. Bob never got involved and would say something to Mam like, 'The weather isn't bad.' He always avoided any mention of money.

While life at the market was always busy, life on a personal level was good too. After marrying, Margaret and I set up our first home on the north side of the city in Parklands, where we had some great neighbours, among them our next-door neighbour Tim Murphy, who dug and seeded our front garden before we even moved in. Tim was a true gentleman and we became great friends with him and his wife Eileen, as well as with the O'Neills, the O'Mahonys and the Varians.

In 1983 and 1985, the two other jewels in my life were born, Sarah and Emma. I became and still am the protective dad. In 1986, we reluctantly left Parklands, as it was on the wrong side of the city for our families and for work. We moved to Willowbank in Blackrock, where we spent twenty wonderful years. Being central to the city centre, the schools and our parents, the location was ideal. As well as that, most of our neighbours had children the same age as ours and so all of us made many friends there.

Right up until the late 1990s, since the time I joined Mam and Paul in the fish stall, the three of us had always been on the go. But we enjoyed our free time too. While I had a passion for motorbikes, Paul always loved driving and was big into cars, ever since he was a teenager. He took every Monday off work and I took Wednesdays. Both of us bought caravans in Garryvoe and spent much time there with our families during the summer months. We went on foreign holidays too, all over the world.

Every Friday, Mam treated herself to a hair-do, either at Tony Bernard's in Princes Street or at home. She still loved Garryvoe as much as ever, and usually went down on a Friday night with Dad for the weekend, as she took every Saturday off. Some years before, Wally O'Brien decided to sell the caravan park in Garryvoe where we had our caravan. Mam was disappointed and said, 'That would be awful Wally. Somebody could ruin it on us. It might never again be the same.' She got it into her head to buy the caravan park, spoke to Dad about it, asked Wally to name his price and bought it there and then. She was chuffed with herself as she loved Garryvoe with all her heart and didn't want it spoiled in any way.

As well as going to Garryvoe often, Mam and Dad travelled further afield too, always with a few friends, on foreign holidays organised by Delaney's hurling and football club. Mam adored the sun and enjoyed meeting people, whether in Thailand, the Far East or on a cruise ship. She had a special fondness for Jersey and went back there time and time again. Whenever she went abroad, she took along a spare suitcase to store all her purchases, usually ornaments or mementos. She was obsessed with phones and collected them in every shape, size and colour. Once, she brought back a wooden phone resembling the street cars in San Francisco, with a wooden ear-piece the size of a plank on top. She installed it at home as her landline.

One day, during a memorable trip to Italy, Mam and Dad were strolling around Naples doing some sightseeing. Mother was wearing a gold cross and chain Dad had bought for her the previous Christmas when two guys tried to rob her. One of them tried to grab the cross and chain. Now, Kathleen was not a big woman, but she had been reared in a pub, ran a market stall and spent her life at fish auctions and so the poor Italian found himself tackling something akin to a Rottweiler. He and his accomplice ended up running down the street, chased by the police, who had been drawn to the scene by all the screaming and shouting. After each holiday, she told every single detail of the trip to her customers at the market and kept raving on about her vacation until she went away again.

All in all, by the late 1990s, the whole family seemed to be in a good place. Paul and I were both happily married, with two children each. Dad was on the verge of retirement. As always, Mam was full of the joys of life and took huge pleasure in fussing over her grandchildren, Sarah, Emma, Eoin and Seán. But then, our world began to fall apart.

7

The Secret

In the late 1990s, I felt that Mam just wasn't the same. Most nights, she went to bed early and seemed to be losing weight. She argued a lot with Dad too. Sometimes, she shook her head, walked away from him and said, 'All picture and no sound.' As time went on, the silences grew longer. Often, she headed off on her own to Garryvoe, while Dad stayed at home alone.

Some days, I wondered if Dad had ever felt left out, especially as Mam, Paul and I worked beside each other all day. Maybe, as the years went on, the dynamics of their marriage had changed. Maybe he had tired of always being in Mam's shadow, even though they were soul mates, like two peas in a pod, and seemed to complement each other. He might have felt too that he had little to give her, as she was so independent in every way.

Yet it was obvious that Mam was unwell. One day, she fainted in the market. When I went to Garryvoe one Sunday, I found she was suffering from a feeling of weakness. Alarm bells started ringing in the back of my brain and I said to myself, 'There's something wrong here.' That evening, when I went home, I said to Dad, 'There's something not right with Mam.' He said, 'I'll talk to her and find out.'

But even though Mam was outgoing, she was private in many ways too. There were certain things we could never discuss with her. Dad failed to get to the root of the problem and said, 'She's just tired.' Paul believed him.

One Sunday in May 1998 I arrived in Garryvoe to be greeted by a very concerned Paul. Mother had again collapsed and despite his best efforts she refused to see a doctor. An hour of my similar efforts had the same result. I drove back to Cork and told Dad of my now very deep concern about Mam's health. Dad and I drove back down to Garryvoe and brought Mam, despite her ongoing arguments, to Dr Murphy who had a practice next door to us at home. He admitted her to hospital.

When we visited her, she told us she had stomach ulcers. Paul and Dad believed her. I didn't. One day, I challenged her. But I had to back down, as she became so upset and insisted that she was telling the truth. I still didn't believe her. After coming out of hospital, she went back to the market. She got weaker and weaker and went back to hospital for more treatment.

As I was seeing her every day, I hadn't spotted how much she had changed, until somebody showed me a recent photograph of her, taken at the stall. I was shocked and could see that she had fallen away to nothing. She got worse and worse and ended up in the South Infirmary for, supposedly, more tests. When she came home, she went straight to bed.

On 13 August, on my forty-first birthday, I rang my aunt Noreen, as we were always close. I said, 'Noreen, I don't believe what the doctor is telling us.' She said, 'We were all told the same Pat.' She advised me to ring the doctor at the South Infirmary.

When I spoke to him, I said, 'I don't believe what you're telling my mother.' He replied, 'I can't tell you.' I said, 'That's rubbish. It's obvious there is something seriously wrong that we don't know about. And I'm going to find out, even if I have to do a song and dance in your waiting room.' He agreed to see me and Noreen. When I told Dad, he said, 'By all means go up.'

On that Thursday, when Noreen and I met the doctor, he told us the truth. He said Mam had asked him not to tell anybody and that he would tell us only if we promised not to let her know that we knew. The news was shocking, much worse than we expected. Mam had stomach cancer and it had spread everywhere. My world fell apart. Then, I thought of Dad and Paul. How would I tell them?

When we went home, I called them both into the kitchen and told them together. They were in bits, shell-shocked. I felt really upset for Paul. Sometimes, he comes across as the tough guy. But underneath, he's a softie and was always the pet in the family. He became very emotional. Then all the questions set in. Did she know how long she had left? I hadn't asked the doctor, as I was so shocked with the news that I couldn't think straight. Why had she kept it to herself? Was it because she didn't want us worrying, or was it her only way of coping?

On the following Friday morning, Paul, Dad and I were in the kitchen, sitting around the table, while Marian, Paul's wife, stayed in the bedroom with Mam. Marian called us and said, 'There's a change in her.' When we went in, she was gone. We stood at her bedside in disbelief, shaken to the core. The woman who had been the centre of our lives, so full of beans until recently, had died. We couldn't accept it. She was only sixty-four and we expected her to live into her eighties at least. We were inconsolable.

Mam was buried in St Michaels in Blackrock. At the time our family grave was in St Josephs but we were informed this was full. St Michaels was the next option but when I went down to pick out the grave I was told in no uncertain terms that the next available grave was in the middle of a row. I explained politely that Kathleen did not like mid-rows. Whether it was mass, a show at the opera house or a meeting, Kathleen always sat on the outside. I was told in this instance she may not notice. Mam was buried in St Michaels graveyard in Blackrock. Her grave is on the outside of the row.

For ages after, when I'd go into the market, I'd expect to see her there, standing behind the counter, dressed in her white nylon coat, with her hair done to perfection, always on the move, emptying boxes of fish, smiling and chatting to the early-morning customers, serving three at a time, full of the joys of life.

Her passing left an awful void in our lives. And, when she died, a little bit of Dad died too.

8

Life without Kathleen

In times of trouble, we quickly find out who our friends are.
With Mam's passing, the outpouring of goodwill and offers
of help from our staff, fellow stall holders, family, friends and
customers were overwhelming and clearly gave a measure of
just how popular Mam had been, how she had touched the
lives of so many people and the high esteem with which she
was held in her native city. Of course, we also heard a lot of
nasty stuff from the begrudgers. But I learned a long time ago
that it's a very long road that doesn't have a turn, so I let the
begrudgers to their own gods.

In hindsight, it's strange but one of my mother's favourite
sayings was, 'The show must go on.' And following her death, it
was very much a case of the business must go on. With a death
in any family, there has to be a time for grieving. Yet looking
back, the business played such a big part in our lives that we
really seemed to be thrown back in at the deep end the week
after Mam's passing.

At all times, Mam had been very much the boss and had a
character that was larger than life. So with Mam gone, Paul
and I had to have a big re-think on how we did business and
look at our individual roles within that structure. As both of us

have strong personalities, we knew that working together as partners in the business would have its difficulties. Should we continue to run two separate stalls under the one umbrella, or should we join the two stalls together?

So for three months or more, the business became all-consuming. Every minute of every day seemed to be taken up with meeting accountants or banks or solicitors or business friends to figure out the best way to maintain what was and is a great legacy. During this period, we had no time for grieving. Looking back, it must have been four or five months later that this huge sense of loss descended on me. I remember one night taking my dog for a walk in the park, down the road from where we live, sitting on a bench and just crying my eyes out. However, it's at times like that I realise that I've picked up more of my mother's traits than I care to admit, because I know she often had moments like that. But, after ten minutes or so, her reaction would always be, 'Cop yourself on, pick yourself up, dust yourself down and get on with it.'

As mentioned earlier, Paul always gives the impression of being the tough guy in our family, always a bit more quick-tempered, always a bit more fiery. And yet, underneath the mask, he is a real softie, a guy who would faint walking in the door of a hospital, a kind of big, cuddly bear. For months after Mam's death, the pain, the upset and sadness was etched on his face.

And then, of course, there was Dad. Mam had always been larger than life. When she was around, there was never a dull moment. She was always changing things, making changes to the house, changing the car, booking a holiday, planning a night out, changing the caravan, whatever, but always changing. Nine times out of ten, Dad would know nothing about any changes she was making until he came home from holidays and found that the windows in the house were different, or that the car was changed. And, because he could be fiery and stubborn, Paul and I waited with baited breath to see his reaction. Often we ended up with a month of what Mother used to call, 'All picture and no sound.'

So when Mam died, it was like somebody drove over Dad with a steam roller and squeezed the very life out of him. In many ways, when Mam passed away, a little bit of my dad died with her.

Paul and I did our best to keep him busy. We involved him as much as possible in the business, either by collecting or delivering fish. We took him out at weekends and called over home almost every evening. Every single day, his sister Noreen and his brother Paul visited him. Sometimes, Noreen went two or three times a day. But I think everybody knew that he was just going through the motions.

Shortly after Mam's passing, Paul and I decided that running two stalls was causing too many problems from a logistics point of view. If one of us was ill or had to attend a meeting, covering for the other was difficult. So, we decided to knock the wall between us, re-tile my area to match Paul's side and work together as one. Although we are very different in personality, we've always worked well with each other and manage to blend our ideas together, rather than pull in opposite directions. After about two years, I made up my mind to modernise, as I was unhappy with the overall appearance of the stall, which still had a look of two halves about it, rather than of one complete unit.

One afternoon, during a day of torrential rain, Paul and his brother in-law Denis, who had joined our staff, were checking something on the computer in the office when there was an almighty rumble overhead. Paul shouted at Denis to get out of the office. They were so lucky because no sooner had they stepped out than the whole ceiling collapsed. I can only describe it as a tsunami. Later, we found out that the gutters, which were about a metre deep and half a metre wide and ran the whole length of the market, were unable to cope with the heavy downpour. As the gutters were internal, they ran directly over our unit and, due to the huge volume of water, they simply collapsed, sending a deluge of water into the office and out into the stall. The damage and destruction was overwhelming. We lost our entire stock of fish. Our electrics, cabinets, fridge, counter, fax machine, telephone and documentation were all destroyed and a plant stall beside us was slightly damaged. The cost of the repair came to about €150,000. But instead of becoming depressed or upset, I convinced myself that Mam was letting us know that it was time to revamp.

Deep down, I wanted to put my own and Paul's stamp on any renovation. Both of us had strong ideas on what we wanted, yet we had to be so careful to maintain the legacy, character and tradition of what we had already.

To get things moving, we got in touch with Horaldo de Oliveira, a Brazilian architect who lived in Cork and whose work I had seen and admired. I knew that he could see outside the box and, between Horaldo, Paul and myself, we thrashed out the new design.

Then the fun started. As we couldn't close down the stall during the renovations, we decided to do the revamp in two sections. As it was such a different design from the original – the ceiling is unlike anything else in the market – we incurred delays at every step along the way. Also, trying to work around builders is difficult at the best of times, but trying to run a food business with work in progress became a living nightmare. On top of that, customers could see some of the work as it developed and their mixed reviews on the design and the dark wood ceiling seriously battered my confidence. But all credit to Paul and my wife Margaret, as neither of them ever uttered a word of doubt.

Just as the project was nearing completion, I came in one morning to find water shooting up at the new ceiling. The mains at the back had burst and we ended up having to hack up the floor. As if that wasn't bad enough, the vibrations of the kango hammer cracked the old cast-iron pipes, which meant we had to take out a section of the roof. Thankfully, when all the pieces finally came together, the finished stall turned out to be iconic.

Later that year, the stall won the best shop front in Cork in its class, and the best overall shop front in Cork, both great awards for a market stall.

However, the biggest compliment of all came from my father, who had been very sceptical during the revamp. Half-way through, we'd had a very bad argument, during which he went ballistic at the cost of the refurbishment and the way it was turning out. Shortly after the stall was finished, we were having lunch one Sunday at Garryvoe Hotel. When talk inevitably turned to business, he said, 'Son, you were right and I was wrong and you definitely have your mother's belief and stubbornness.' That was the best compliment I could have got.

As time went on, Dad's words of praise become even more precious to me, especially when I came to realise that, sadly, his life was drawing to a close.

9

A Man of Style and Dignity

Dad being Dad was always a very private man. Like most men, he never talked much about his health or health concerns. So in 2002, when Paul and I found out that he was getting up quite a bit at night to go to the bathroom, alarm bells started ringing.

Under orders, he went to his doctor and was referred to a specialist after some blood tests. I went along to the specialist with him and was glad to find that the consultant happened to be a customer of ours, Dermot Lannigan, a really nice guy. However, the prognosis was not good, as Dad was diagnosed with prostate cancer which, apparently, he had ignored for a long time.

Over the next two years, we went through a see-saw of emotions, with good days, bad days and sometimes downright awful days. We lived from the result of one blood test to the next, from one specialist appointment to the next and from one hospital visit to the next. Deep down, we all knew that, no matter how brave a face Dad put on it, the cancer was taking its toll. I suppose when you are dealing with people all your life, you become good at reading body language and facial expressions. This became invaluable when dealing with Dad. Whenever somebody asked him about how he was feeling, he always replied, 'Oh I'm grand.' Paul and I quickly learned to read the signs. Was he limping slightly? Was he a bit tetchy? Was he a bit pale? Did he have breakfast? Some days, the pain was so intense that he could not move.

During all of Dad's illness, the family rallied round and Paul and I will never be able to put into words our eternal gratitude to Dad's sister Noreen, his brother Paul, our wives Marian and Margaret, and everyone who helped along the way.

Yet even with all that invaluable help, we were struggling and felt way out of our depth. On Christmas eve, this became painfully obvious. Dad came into the market and even though he tried to disguise it, I noticed that he was limping. When I asked Paul if he had noticed it too, he said he had just asked Dad how he was feeling and Dad had answered, 'I'm fine.'

At about 3.00 p.m., Dad left the market to go home for a rest, which had become part of his daily routine. After work, I usually went home, had dinner, showered, popped over to see Dad and watched Sky Sports with him, or Paul went instead. But on Christmas eve, I went straight over to Dad's house, as something had been niggling me about that limp since earlier in the day. I found Dad crouched on the bed, in so much pain that he couldn't even reach to pick up the phone to call one of us. Straight away, I rang for an ambulance. After a heated discussion, Dad was taken to the Bon Secours hospital. The ambulance driver was under the instruction to take him to the Cork University Hospital or to the South Infirmary. I argued that his records and his doctor were at the Bon Secours. It was an argument I had no intention of losing.

This time, it took Dad a lot longer to bounce back. We needed reinforcements and they appeared in the form of home-care nurses from Marymount hospice. Never in my life have I come across such a helpful, resourceful, caring, dedicated bunch of people. They called to Dad under the guise of public health nurses, as I didn't want to terrify him with the mention of the hospice. Their arrival, even though Paul and I didn't realise it at the time, heralded a new stage. Very quickly, the emphasis changed to pain management, and not if the cancer would kill Dad but when. With the Marymount nurses on board, there seemed to be a strange calmness to all this. Everything seemed to be controlled and managed. When we asked questions, we got honest, pragmatic answers. The nurses managed Dad's tablets, which amounted to twenty-eight tablets daily. And, miracle of miracles, they got information from him without any trouble.

One evening, about two months after the home-care team had started their visits, Dad and I were sitting down watching Sky Sports. When I asked him who had called that morning, he said, 'Noreen called at about ten o'clock and we had a cup of tea. The Marymount nurse came around two o'clock and Noreen popped in again about five o'clock for a few minutes.' Surprised at what he had said, I asked, 'What Marymount nurse?' He smiled and replied, 'Oh the one you describe as the public health nurse.' Sheepishly, I asked, 'When did you find out?' He laughed and said, 'The very first day she called.' When I asked why he hadn't told me, he replied, 'Because the nurse said it was a secret.'

One thing I've learned about serious illness is that it can bring a frankness and clarity to conversations, attitudes and perspectives that would normally be avoided. I remember having long conversations with Mam in her last few weeks when we were alone, about things that, even though we were always very close, she would never ever have discussed with me. During Dad's illness, I became a lot closer to him. Paul always seemed much more relaxed with Dad. Maybe I respected him too much or thought he expected more from me, being the eldest. Often, I think back to a school report in my early days at Coláiste Chríost Rí, in which I got the highest mark in the class in history, the only time I think I ever got the highest mark in anything. My marks in maths though weren't great and I remember Dad's reaction, 'There's room for a lot of improvement in maths.'

From the moment Marymount came on board, I had this nightmare of having to explain to Dad that he would need to go into the hospice at some stage. As it turned out, when the time came, I think he was quite happy to go in, as he felt totally secure there and relaxed in their care.

As far as I am concerned, the likes of Sister Marcella, Sister Nan, the doctors and staff of Marymount are all living saints. To me, their work could never be described as a job, but rather as an absolute vocation.

In the hospice, Dad proved to be an unusual patient. He refused to stay in bed. Instead, he got up, dressed, strolled around, chatted to the nurses and other patients or sat in the hall waiting for Paul, myself, Marian or Margaret to visit.

One night, as Dad's brother Paul and I were leaving the hospice, Paul said that he couldn't understand why Dad got up and dressed every single day he possibly could. But that was just Dad's way of fighting cancer.

Of course, the inevitable happened. In 2004, Dad passed away. A few weeks later, I went up to Marymount to thank Sister Marcella and the staff for all their help and support. I got talking to one of the staff and she told me that they had great admiration for the way Dad had battled his illness. I agreed but said, 'He didn't beat it.' She answered, 'Few do. But, he had a style and a dignity all of his own.'

In my heart, I wish I had been closer to my dad. Yet I can honestly say that I was always desperately proud of him. I think that day I knew why, as he did indeed have a style and a dignity all of his own.

10

Easy Rider

My earliest memories of two-wheel transport go all the way back to when my dad had a scooter. I vaguely recall standing in front of him on a blue Vespa when I was three years old and Mam sitting on the back. But it was Dad's brother Paul who really got me excited about bikes.

When I was about ten years of age, Uncle Paul owned what I thought at the time was the most beautiful motorcycle ever made, a red Jawa 350. Often dressed in his shiny, black leather jacket, he would whisk me off for a short spin on the back of his bike. Awesome. Even then, I could sense the freedom and adventure a bike had to offer. Although, if my mother only knew the number of times Uncle Paul had taken me for a ride, she would surely have put a stop to it all.

Years later, when I started at CIT, Dad bought me a Honda 50, which came in handy, as otherwise I would have had to hop on two buses to get to college. Even though it was only a run around, I was bitten by the motorbike bug and relished the sense of freedom I felt as I zoomed every day from Friar's Walk out to Bishopstown and back. The bike became useful too for delivering fish parcels.

Later, I moved on to a Honda 70 and began to get ideas that a 250 or a 500 might soon be on the cards. In my head, I began to plan trips to Wales and Scotland. But then, on my twenty-first birthday, I got a present of a Fiesta and two-wheel transport ended up on the back shelf.

Much later in life, one of my daughters became friends with the son of Chris Royal, a motorbike dealer. Suddenly, what had always been an interest now became much more attractive. The inevitable happened of course and, being in my forties, I could always claim that I was suffering a serious mid-life crisis. So I went for a snoop around Chris' showrooms. On the spot, I fell for a Suzuki 800 Cruiser. There and then, Chris and I struck a deal. The bike turned out to be simply awful. I found it really uncomfortable and its suspension proved hard going on an already delicate back. After about a month, I mustered up the courage to go back to Chris and explain the situation. He recommended a Bandit 1200, which was the same value, and so I went with his advice.

To my amazement, Margaret took a shine to the Bandit and enjoyed nothing more than going off for a blast on it on a Sunday evening. We were like two teenagers again, as free as the wind. Naturally, my teenage dreams surfaced once more and in no time at all we were touring all around Wales, England and France.

After a short while, I bought my dream bike, a BMW1200 RT. It was such an incredible machine that I thought I had died and gone to heaven. But the beauty of the bike was that parking it in the city cost nothing, whereas parking a car in the city cost about €20 each day. So not only was I fulfilling my passion, but I was also cutting costs.

As soon as we got the chance, Margaret and I toured all over Europe. We adored France, apart from the motorways, which were great for making time but otherwise boring. While I admire the French for their appreciation of food, I believe that Ireland's produce is so much better. Italy won me over too, a fabulous place to visit, and the Italians have such flair and style.

In Germany, the people were efficient and meticulous. Almost everything ran on time, but often I found the rules and regulations stifling. And I quickly learned that Germans don't like motorbikes filtering. In Oberstaufen, on the German-Swiss border, Margaret and I got lectured for wearing shorts by an elderly man in the sauna in our hotel. Seemingly, in that part of the world, nudity is the norm in the sauna. Considering that this very elderly man was accompanied by two very elderly women, I responded by saying that maybe they too should wear shorts. Apart from a sense of stiff regulation, Germany itself is magnificent.

In Belgium, we loved Brugge, with its lovely, cobbled streets, unique atmosphere and magical displays of traditional foods in artisan shops, many of which are family-run. Its old buildings impressed me too, especially the fact that great use was made of them.

To date, our biggest trip has been to the west coast of America. In any part of the world, being Irish is great, but particularly in America. Our ability to laugh at most situations and not to take ourselves too seriously must surely be one of our greatest traits. In January, in the midst of a miserable Irish winter, we booked our bike from Eagle Rider Motorcycle Rentals in Las Vegas. In July, when we touched down in Las Vegas to collect the bike, it was melting. Having filled in all the paper work for the bike, the guy at EagleRider asked us what route we were taking, as we were leaving the bike in San Diego, not Las Vegas. We told him about our plan to ride through the Mojave Desert, up to San Francisco and down route 101 to San Diego. He stood there and stared at us in silence for quite a while before he politely told us that Harleys are air cooled and operate up to 120 degrees, but that temperatures in the Mojave Desert could easily soar to up to 135 degrees at that time of year. He warned us that if the bike broke down in the desert, there was no way that EagleRider would collect it there. Sometimes, ignorance is bliss and to this day Margaret and I still laugh when we think of the look on the guy's face as we rode away.

So off to the Mojave Desert we went. We spent two nights in the most aptly named place we ever visited, Furnace Creek. The shimmering haze reduced visibility there to a short distance. Tumbleweeds rolled by in the scorching breeze. Every few miles, water tanks were on hand to top up the radiators of cars to avoid over-heating. Apparently, most bikers ride through Furnace Creek at night. Was it incredible? Yes. Was it terrifying? Yes. Would we do it again? Doubtful. Are we glad we did it? Oh yes.

During that trip, we mixed the accommodation. But we decided to treat ourselves in San Francisco and so we booked into the Hilton Hotel. When we pulled up outside the door, the parking attendant looked at us as if to say, 'These two must have the wrong hotel.' It was truly the trip of a lifetime.

Back home, a group of us oldies go for a bike trip most Sunday mornings. Usually, we ride out of Cork at about 8.00 a.m. and arrive back around 1.00 p.m. More often than not, we head west, stop for a long coffee, sort out the world's problems in five minutes, have a laugh and just relax. Originally, we met up through our love of bikes and we all seem to be really comfortable in each other's company. It's a great way to unwind, enjoy the moment and forget about business for a while.

Yet, despite all our travel and the wonderful places we've seen, I love coming home. Ireland is such a super country, with excellent food, fantastic people, a great sense of fun and no climate extremes.

11

Talking Shop

Since 1990, I have been a committee member of the Market Traders Association, to which most of the English Market stall holders belong. The association holds regular meetings where traders' grievances and ideas are exchanged and discussed. Events and strategies for the market are debated and planned, and the fruits of these discussions are then brought by the committee members to City Council, which was formerly known as Cork Corporation, and Irish Estates, who run the day-to-day affairs of the market on behalf of City Council.

I suppose, like all businesses, matters of finance, such as rents, service charges and capital expenditure, are the ones that tend to have the most heated dialogue on all sides. At times, exchanges have reached boiling point during rent reviews, especially when we traders hear of unrealistic and illogical comparisons of market rents paid on Cork's main shopping street, Patrick Street. This was particularly true during the Celtic Tiger years.

In recent years, I've noted with some satisfaction that the discussions have moved very much away from confrontation to ones of co-operation and compromise. People such as Valerie O'Sullivan, Paul Moynihan, Damien O'Mahony, Alison

O'Rourke, Jim O'Donovan, and our present and recent lord mayors, seem to have a better understanding of how the market works and that its true value to Cork city cannot be measured by its rent role. They have encouraged dialogue and have been proactive in developing and promoting the market. I think that the queen's visit and events such as culture nights are excellent examples of this co-operation. The English Market has a vital role to play in attracting tourists to this stunning city. The City Council, Irish Estates and the traders have an important part to play in ensuring the market is protected in its present form as a living, working, thriving food market. To me, that is the next challenge. It can only be achieved through understanding, discussion and co-operation. On this one, we all need to be singing from the same hymn sheet.

I am also a member of Retail Excellence Ireland. With over one thousand retail companies involved, REI is the largest retail industry trade body in Ireland. It aims to enhance the consumers' retail experience by developing excellent retail standards and skills. Obviously, these aims and objectives fit our business model exceptionally well. The association is a strong and efficient lobby for its members, and David Fitzsimons, its chief executive officer, is highly articulate in promoting the association's concerns and ideas.

Regularly, REI run interesting forums and arrange trips both in Ireland and abroad to highlight best practice in a variety of businesses. The Food Store in Claremorris is a recent example of one of these field trips; a striking food shop built and operated on traditional values, but with a very modern twist. The ideas bounced around on that visit were both practical and challenging. Also, REI provides constant training opportunities for its members and advice from experts in a range of fields is only a phone call or an e-mail away.

For many years, I have also been a member of Good Food Ireland. I am a big fan of its leading lady, Margaret Jeffares. Margaret's ability to market Irish quality food is incredible. Good Food Ireland embodies everything that is good about Irish food and I am proud to be a member of such a prestigious organisation.

The remainder of my very scarce time is given to the Cork Business Association. The CBA does great work on behalf of its members, lobbying council and government on issues ranging from rates to parking, derelict buildings, festivals, traffic flow and busking. Its remit is huge and I often wonder how such a small organisation can cope so well with such a massive workload, but it does.

Clearly, the organisations of which we are members make a strong statement as to where we want our business to be – at the top. Even on holidays, whether in Ireland or abroad, I love browsing around fish shops, looking at different displays, counters and prices, chatting to fishmongers and seeing how they serve their customers. I love Italy, France and Spain, as I always seem to learn something there. A few years ago in Spain, I first saw the sealable bags we use these days. It took a while to track them down, but track them down I did. In our business, water and electronics are always a problem. There was a time when we were forever having trouble with water getting into our counter-top weighing scales. That was until I spotted a suspended, digital scales in Italy. Now, that's what we use. No matter what ideas I see elsewhere, I always try to adapt them to our own tradition and style in the market. However, from what I have seen abroad, the quality and variety of fish that this island nation has to offer are much superior to that of any other country.

In recent years, my daughter Emma and Paul's son Seán started working with us in the market. Their entry into the business marks yet another generation of O'Connells there. For Paul and myself, the timing couldn't be better, as we have expanded the business with the addition of a new smokehouse in Bandon. This has been a major investment for the business, but Paul has always wanted to smoke our own produce. He has pursued this with fervour and passion. Now, his dedication and time are paying off handsomely, as what he is producing is second to none. He uses only wild or organic salmon and smokes it in a time-honoured traditional way, with nothing added except a little salt, oak smoke and time. Also, he produces wonderful, naturally-smoked haddock and fabulous smoked trout. I am very proud of what he has achieved in Bandon in such a short space of time and I'm very proud of the product he is producing. Of course, without our staff rallying around and covering Paul's work in Bandon, none of this would be possible. But, as I've said before, we seem to be one big family anyway.

While we recognise the vast contribution our staff has made to the success of our business, so too we have great respect and admiration for the fishermen who supply us.

12

The Seafarer

Recently, I attended a lunch at the Rochestown Park Hotel in Cork for the Cork Person of the Year, a wonderful celebration of people who have in some way made a major contribution to the life and community of the city and county. On this particular day, the prestigious award was given to the Union Hall community, who were so involved and gave so much of their time to the search and recovery of the bodies of five crew members of the *Tit Bonhomme* trawler, which tragically sank after hitting Adam Island in Glandore Harbour early on 15 January 2012. On behalf of the community, the local parish priest Father Pierce Cormac accepted the award, along with Bill Deasy, a man whose veins must surely be filled with seawater rather than blood at this stage, as he has been so much a part of fishing in Union Hall.

While I was absolutely thrilled that the village of Union Hall got recognition for its heroic efforts in recovering the bodies, somehow I felt that such acknowledgement must have felt utterly inadequate for the families and loved ones of those who had lost their lives.

Naturally, being a fishmonger keeps me close to the fishing communities of Cork. On the whole, I find that fishermen tend to be highly independent, have a strong work ethic and a firm belief in the dignity of hard work and of supporting themselves, their families and their communities. In places like Union Hall and Castletownbere, many come from multi-generational fishing families. Fishing is in their blood. At times, we might argue over price or quality or the days they land their fish, yet I have nothing but the greatest admiration for these men. Along with the fishing industry, they are the life blood of many small towns and villages in our coastal areas. Unfortunately, it's highly unlikely a Dell or an Apple factory will ever be seen in these regions. So these fishermen and the fishing industry are vital to these communities.

However, at times I feel that the people of small fishing villages are treated like a disenfranchised or forgotten group. In my heart, I'm convinced that when politicians visit areas like Glandore or Union Hall during the summer months, they see these places as well-to-do holiday villages, full of bustle and activity. But they have no idea of life there in the depths of winter, nor do they understand the extent to which these villages are dependent on a thriving, sustainable fishing industry. And yet, these same politicians make decisions from Dublin and Brussels on quotas, fishing regulations and grants, sometimes with catastrophic results, as happened in the 1970s, seemingly because the fishing industry was sidelined in favour of agriculture, which had a much stronger lobby.

In my view, fishing should always have been regarded as one of our greatest natural resources. For so many years now, our marine policies have been just aspirational goals rather than achievable targets. And politicians have been put in charge of marine policy as a sort of a reward, or for constituency reasons, instead of for their knowledge or experience in sea-related matters.

As fishing is an inherently dangerous occupation, it has always had its tragedies. But the danger has in no way been lessened by successive governments who, sometimes with the best of intentions but not always with enough knowledge or enough foresight, have put fishermen under greater economic pressure due to quotas, restrictions and the high cost of diesel, with apparently little understanding of the effects these changes have on the fishing industry.

When you are involved with the fishing communities, it's easy to see how grief, sadness and a sense of loss can quickly turn to anger in these small, often isolated, areas. Every single loss at sea affects so many people in little, close-knit communities – wives or partners, sons, daughters, parents, relations and friends.

On the back of our stall, we had a wonderful photograph of a fisherman in his oilskins, working on the deck of the *Pierre Charles* from Dunmore East. He was totally engrossed in his job and his face had a lifetime of the sea etched into it. Sadly, he lost his life recently at sea.

Down through the years, we bought a lot of fish at the auctions in Helvick Head in Waterford, and so we got to know the locals well, among them Cáitlín Uí hAodha. I remember when Cáitlín got her skipper's licence, you could almost touch the pride of the little community there. Cáitlín's husband Michael Hayes was the skipper of the *Tit Bonhomme* and tragically lost his life when the trawler went down only a few minutes from safety. Anyone who has heard the last, frantic moments on board that boat, as the crew desperately phoned for help, would very quickly understand the inherent dangers of fishing. Although the *Tit Bonhomme* was in plain sight of home, it still couldn't be saved. And so, the list goes on and on. Do we admire and respect these fishermen? People involved in the fish trade certainly do, but the rest of the people on this island of ours? Probably not half enough.

13

People in High Places

Over the years, the English Market has played host to many personalities from the world of politics, food, fashion, theatre, music, television, sport and cinema. Presidents, monarchs, ambassadors, ministers, movie stars and celebrity chefs have all visited. The list is endless. When these people drop in, there is always a bit of a buzz about the place. But for me, the real bonus is that they always leave with a sense of Cork – its fun, its slagging and its ability to laugh at itself.

Yet no matter who pops by, I am always aware that first and foremost I am a fishmonger. I sell fish for a living. Also, I promote the English Market, as I feel especially lucky to have worked in and been a part of the market for most of my life. I also view the English Market as being an important factor of Cork's history, particularly due to its folklore and its character, as well as its effect on the local economy. The market plays a huge role in making Cork such a city of welcomes. And, because it has welcomed so many visitors, the traders of the market have taken on the role of unofficial ambassadors for Cork, ensuring that each and every visitor gets the warmest of welcomes.

For me, the English Market stands as a great example of how small, indigenous family-run businesses can survive in a city centre. For this reason, it is highly unlikely that I would ever be rude, nasty or intolerant of any of the politicians or celebrities who call.

My personal opinion of these people remains just that – personal. On the whole, most of them seem charming and decent anyway. I say this because an associate of mine once slated me for being nice to Mícheál Martin when he paid us a visit soon after his election as leader of Fianna Fáil. I came from the same area as Mícheál, went to the same school as him and have been friends all my life with his brother Seán. So why would I want to abuse or embarrass him in a public place? Despite a lot of personal tragedy, Mícheál keeps bouncing back and I think he was one of the best ministers of education ever.

When Martin McGuinness of Sinn Féin visited our counter on one occasion, and a member of Britain's royal family on another, I treated each of them with the same courtesy and respect. My role as a fishmonger is certainly not to be judgemental of my customers or visitors.

Any time Charles Haughey came to the market, he always made a bit of a stir. A hugely divisive character, he was viewed as either god or the devil himself. With Charlie, there was no in-between. Before his arrival, one of his handlers always rang to say that Charlie was on his way. I felt this was just a way of sussing out what we thought of him. If the handler believed we didn't rate Charlie as god, I think that he would simply have passed us by. But I must have been a good actor, as Charlie always called to us. On each visit, he arrived amid a throng of

Fianna Fáil officials and supporters, with the local Fianna Fáil TDs jostling excitedly for positions next to him. Although small in stature, he had a lord-of-the-manor aura about him and he appeared to command great respect. In hindsight, I wonder if that respect was based on admiration or fear. At all times, he was polite and affable and exuded intelligence. Yet I always sensed an underlying ruthlessness, as if he was in pursuit of what he wanted and out for his own gain.

A likeable guy, Bertie Ahern was charisma personified. Even during his time as taoiseach, I almost felt obliged to call him Bertie. He had an innate ability to be just one of the lads and I can still picture him standing at our counter with an arm around the shoulder, chatting about business, or having a laugh over sport. In the market, he always seemed very much at home with both traders and customers alike. What a pity that his so-called soft landing turned out to be somewhat similar to walking blindfolded into a mine shaft.

On television, Enda Kenny always struck me as being stiff and uncomfortable. Yet when I met him, he was utterly charming. On his visits to the market, he always took time to listen, never rushed away, showed interest in what everyone else had to say and told a story of his own too. He came across as a man who believes in hard work and in the dignity of toil and effort.

Another member of Fine Gael, Simon Coveney, who is doing an excellent job as minister for agriculture, food and the marine, often calls to the market. Whenever I disagree with something he may be doing, I threaten to air-brush him out of the massive photograph hanging in our stall of Queen Elizabeth's visit to the market. Like Simon, Jerry Buttimer, Dara

Murphy, Ciarán Lynch, Deirdre Clune and Kathleen Lynch are all regular visitors and shoppers in the market.

When President Mary McAleese paid us a visit, we had the pleasure of presenting her with a side of smoked Irish salmon. In my mind, she was one of the finest Irish presidents ever. Her work in Northern Ireland and her ability to represent this country abroad at the highest level made everyone proud. She will certainly be a hard act to follow.

Quiet, shy, polite, even ordinary, these are not the words most people would use to describe Oliver Reed. Many will recall his reckless antics on *The Late Late Show* with Gay Byrne, which added greatly to his image and reputation as a hell-raiser. Yet at our counter, he could easily have passed as the local curate, as he was indeed quiet, shy, polite and ordinary. After moving to Churchtown in north Cork, he became a regular customer and he truly was a gentle giant.

When Angela Lansbury, the *Murder She Wrote* actress, and her husband Peter Shaw built a house near Shanagarry in east Cork, they too became regular shoppers at our stall. They made a wonderful couple. A charming man, Peter was easy to get along with and loved east Cork with a passion. Sadly, he passed away some years ago, but we still see Angela. I love the way she seems to blend in with everyone else at our counter, even though she is world famous.

When he isn't gallivanting around some exotic part of the world, Tim Severin, the adventurer and writer, often pops in to buy some fish. Tim lives life to the full and enthrals us with tales of his escapades and descriptions of the places he has visited. Usually, he won't tell where he is off to next as, like most sailors, he's highly superstitious. But we always hear about it when he comes back. A fascinating man and a fascinating life.

Recently, Michael Portillo, who seems to have given up politics for a more adventurous life, recorded a piece on the English Market for his documentary *Great Railway Journeys*. Outside our stall, we set up a table and three chairs, sat down with Michael and chatted casually while we sampled a traditional meal of salt ling, onion and potato, cooked by the ever-obliging Kay Harte from the Farmgate Restaurant. We were having such a laugh that the producer kept trying to hurry us up, as we were running way over time. Poor Michael was parched after the salt fish. So, like any good Cork man, I suggested a pint of – no, not Guinness, as the man was in Cork – Murphy's of course, boy. That particular programme got a huge reaction, seemingly because the area looked so stunning.

To me, Keith Floyd was one of the first celebrity chefs to really add entertainment as a vital ingredient of food. Unannounced, Floyd arrived at our counter with his camera and production crew. He asked my mother if they could film the stall and if she would mind saying a few words. The poor woman was nearly in need of smelling salts at the thought of appearing on television. In those days, television cameras were a rare sight indeed, especially in the market. Mam said she would be terrified and had serious reservations. But Floyd was so laid back and personable that in no time at all the cameras were rolling and Floyd and Mam were having a great old chat. I think that Floyd was one of the first international chefs to sense the magic of the market, and that particular show that he recorded about thirty years ago still makes good viewing.

As it happened, the producer of Floyd's show later worked with Rick Stein. Many years afterwards, when Stein himself was filming *Food Heroes* in the market, he paid us a visit. What a laugh we had, as he's a fabulous guy, with a huge knowledge of fish and cooking. He made what I consider to be one of the best television programmes on the market and it still gets regular showings on television.

To me, though, none of these celebrity chefs can hold a candle to the Allens. From Myrtle to Darina to Rachel, the level to which they have brought Irish food, through their books, television shows and Ballymaloe cookery school, is nothing short of a miracle. Over the years, I have watched them as they have grown Ballymaloe into what it is today, brought out an impressive collection of books and made numerous cookery television programmes, all done tastefully, with slickness and professionalism. They are to me the pinnacle of all that is good in Irish food today, and I consider it an honour to have been featured in many of their shows and to see them in the market on a regular basis.

Another regular caller is the celebrity chef and television personality Neven Maguire. A few years ago, Neven arrived at our counter to buy some Dublin Bay prawns for a cookery demonstration he was giving in Carrigaline. As I picked the prawns and wrapped them, we had a great old banter. To pay for the prawns, Neven passed me €50. I gave him a wink and discreetly handed him back five €10 notes, as we don't charge for small amounts of fish used for cookery demonstrations, especially as it's in our own interest that people learn to cook fish. Anyway, about a year later, Neven happened to be giving a cookery demonstration in aid of my old *alma mater*, Coláiste Chríost Rí. We had agreed to give some sponsorship and so were present on the night. Of course, Neven couldn't resist telling the story about the five €10 notes and the wink. Back at the stall the following morning, every second customer was giving me the wink. I had to explain to them that I had winked at Neven, not the other way round, so they still had to pay.

In Cork sporting circles, few come more renowned than Ronan O'Gara. In Cork, Ronan is a god and for good reason. Ronan is a regular at our counter and a nicer guy you couldn't meet. Cool as a breeze, Ronan loves the slagging he gets in the market; we kind of feel it helps keep his feet on the ground. I've seen Ronan – I'm being very polite here because everyone calls him Rog – time and time again sign autographs or chat with children or their parents at our counter and I've never ever seen him refuse or hurry them in any way. Both himself and Seán Óg Ó hAilpín are outstanding ambassadors for Cork.

All in all, we've had a great mix of high-profile people visiting the market. Yet, it has to be said, the visitor who created the biggest buzz of all was undoubtedly the famous, elderly woman who came from just across the water.

14

The Preparation

In early 2011, Cork was awash with rumours that President Obama was likely to come to University College Cork during his trip to Ireland later that year. To put a plan in place for the expected visit, Cork City Council and UCC worked closely together. However, it soon became obvious that the president's visit to Ireland was going to be extremely brief and that fitting a Cork stopover into to such a tight schedule was totally out of the question.

One day, Paul Moynihan, a senior executive officer in corporate affairs with Cork City Council, had a lightbulb moment and suggested to the lord mayor, Michael O'Connell, that since a lot of preparation had already been done in the hope that President Obama would visit Cork, Queen Elizabeth II should be invited to the city, especially as the queen had also planned a trip to Ireland during that year. The lord mayor sent out the invitation and got a reply within a week to say that the queen would be delighted to visit Cork during her state visit here. Her visit would be the first by a British monarch to the Republic of Ireland since the visit of King George V in 1911, when the whole island of Ireland was still under British rule.

The Preparation

Of course, the minute word of the visit got out, rumour and counter-rumour spread like wildfire. In all, about fifteen places were mentioned as possible locations for a royal visit, among them City Hall, UCC, Cobh and the English Market. Word had it that the queen had already received a present of *Serving a City,* the incredible story of the English Market, painstakingly put together by the O'Driscoll brothers, and that she was keen to visit the market. Naturally, taking into consideration our troubled past as neighbours, everyone began to wonder what kind of reception the queen would receive, or indeed if she would be welcome at all. In his day, my father would have been very much republican in his views. Mam may have looked at things differently, as most of her brothers had worked and lived in England for long spells. Personally, although I think that we are clearly very much shaped by our past, I don't believe for a minute that we should dwell on it. We are a young, educated country, a strong democracy with a young population and we are more than capable of holding our own with any nation. If what we do today makes a genuine difference and improves relations with our neighbours, then let's not be prisoners of our past. We must learn the lessons of our history, but we must make decisions based on our present and future.

One busy Friday afternoon, having just stepped outside our counter to speak to a customer who had recently been unwell, I suddenly found myself in the midst of a large group of very well-dressed people, about thirty in all, led by Paul Moynihan, who was an employee of Cork City Council. Paul introduced me to Edward Young, deputy private secretary to the queen. We all had a chat and a laugh before the group moved on.

What had become a rumour now became very much a reality, and the first thought to enter my head at that moment was, what would Mam think if she knew that Queen Elizabeth II was now likely to visit her stall? At last, the English Market would have the chance to shine to a huge international audience and showcase Ireland's finest fish, meat, fruit, cheeses, vegetables and breads. Although as yet we had no idea what form the visit would take, I hoped that it could be carried off without changing the very character of the market.

After that Friday afternoon, the wheels began to quickly turn. Soon, we learned that the queen would touch down at Cork Airport and visit the English Market, along with the Tyndall National Institute at UCC, which is Ireland's leading microelectronics research centre. The timeframe for both the preparation for the visit and for the visit itself was tight.

Over the coming days and weeks, City Hall set up a series of meetings with traders, An Garda Síochána, Bord Bia, Bord Fáilte and public relations personnel. Paul Moynihan and his colleague Valerie O'Sullivan, a director of services in corporate and external affairs, took a hands-on approach to the planning and organisation of the Cork leg of the trip. The individual traders whose stalls the queen would visit learned of their selection only a few days before the visit. However, from the moment I heard of the visit, I worked on the basis that our stall would be one of those chosen. If it was, we would be prepared. If not, so be it.

For the next month, I prepared for the day of the royal visit. As I've said before, Castletownbere has been very good to our business down through the years. Truly, I believe their fish is among the best in the world. And if we were picked to showcase Irish fish to the world on the day of the visit, then O'Connell's would not be found wanting. For me, it was also important to show the character and tradition of the market, because for centuries, in this little space in the middle of Cork city, everything has changed and yet nothing has changed.

For years, I'd had a copy of a black and white photo taken in the market of Sheehan's fish stall sometime around 1910, showing the two Sheehan brothers who ran the stall, along with their wives and a young child, aged around ten, whom I assume was one of their sons. I got the photo enlarged to about seven feet in height and about fourteen feet in length. My thinking was that, in many ways, the photograph depicted a lot of what is and has been the ethos of the market down through the years – family-run businesses, superb product, hard work and lots of character.

With about two weeks to go to the visit, the market showed a noticeable increase in activity. Bord Bia, Bord Fáilte and An Garda Síochána were now very visible and constantly engaging with the traders and City Council. All of these worked closely with the traders' committee. Due to the short timespan allowed for the preparation, the committee, and its chairman Tom Durcan in particular, were on call around the clock. Peter Kelly – better known as Franc and famous for his wedding programme on RTÉ – was invited in to add a little colour and imagination to the duller areas of the market, though he was under strict instructions not to interfere with its very essence. His imagination, touch and subtlety worked a treat, from placing full grown trees in grey areas to decorating the fountain with a fabulous array of vegetables. Parts of the market that had been hidden away suddenly came to life.

On the Friday before the queen's visit, I got a phone call from Paul Moynihan saying that our stall had been selected as one of the stalls the queen would visit and asking me to attend a meeting on Monday morning in City Hall. My reaction, of course, was what would Kathleen O'Connell have thought had she received that phone call, the woman who had left South Presentation Convent at primary level, took a huge gamble on opening a small fish stall, and that very same stall was now going to receive a visit from Queen Elizabeth II? The other stalls chosen were Ashley O'Neill, butchers; The Farmer, fruit and vegetables; Isabelle Sheridan, cheese and delicatessen; Jerry Moynihan, poultry and eggs; Sheila Fitzpatrick, breads; and Toby Simmonds, olives. The excitement and apprehension around the market was palpable. We were informed that only family and staff would be allowed in on the day and all these people had to fill in questionnaires, which would then be vetted by the relevant authorities.

For the previous five weeks, Paul and I had worked towards the expectation that our stall would probably be one of those the queen would visit. The fact that the expectation would now become a reality started to set off panic attacks. Would we have the fish we needed on the day? How would the visit be received in Cork? And, of course, what the hell do you chat about to the queen? Unfortunately, my knowledge of horses is zilch and I wasn't sure how much the queen knew about fish. Not a great starting point, really.

The Preparation

On Monday, the seven stall holders chosen to meet the queen arrived at City Hall as arranged. There, we met the lord mayor Michael O'Connell, Tim Lucey the city manager, an official from the British Embassy, Valerie O'Sullivan, Paul Moynihan and members of An Garda Síochána. We were told about the order of the queen's visit, the entrance through which she would arrive, areas where presentations would be made, lengths of the visit and the time she would spend at each stall. Also, we were informed of the protocol involved, part of which suggested that we would stand behind our counters while speaking to the queen. Sheila Fitzpatrick and I objected to this, as we felt that greeting the queen from behind the counter would create an immediate barrier. For my part, if I was showcasing Irish fish, I wanted to be able to pick up the different varieties of fish, not only to show them to the queen, but also to the worldwide audience looking on. We were told that it would be highly unlikely that we would be allowed to speak to the queen from outside the counter. But thirty minutes later, after a review of the situation, we were told that one trader at each of the selected stalls could stand outside the counter to greet the queen. Even then, I sensed that this was a hugely important decision.

Over the next few days, arrangements were put in place for bringing in stock before Friday, the day of the visit, as only people who had been vetted and had identity cards on the day would be allowed in. That week, security was tight and everyone was busy putting the final pieces in place. From a personal point of view, the pressure was intense. I suppose, compared to other products available in the market, ours is the most volatile supply-wise. We are weather dependent and also need a bit of luck with regards to the right catch on any given day. As it turned out, on that particular week, luck was on our side. On Thursday, the day before the visit, our fridge was heaving with the best fish this country has to offer, from stunning cod to perfect prawns.

At 5.30 p.m., members of An Garda Síochána carried out a security check on all the stalls, fridges and offices in the market. As our fridge was literally full to the brim, it meant that they had to empty the fridge first, check the boxes and then refill it. As Paul opened the fridge, he said to the three gardaí present, 'Ye really picked the short straw here lads.' I have to say, their professionalism was a credit to the force. But throughout the entire preparation, that was the case with everyone involved.

At 6.30 p.m., on the eve of the queen's visit, all the English Market traders closed their stalls and left the market as requested. I went home, looking forward to a good night's rest. But it wasn't to be, as I never slept a wink.

15

The Visit of Queen Elizabeth II

The night before the visit had turned out to be frustrating. All night long, I twisted and turned. My mind refused to relax. Deep down, what was really bothering me of course was the fact that there would be no re-takes, no second chances. In the English Market, the traders are well used to being in front of cameras. But the big difference this time was that there would be only one opportunity to get it right. I would have only three or four minutes with the queen. The world would be watching and watching closely. If anything went wrong, there would be no chance to say, 'We'll re-do that last piece.'

During the previous week, I'd obviously considered the possibilities of how my conversation with the queen might go. The trouble was that I had no idea what the queen was like. If I'm honest, she always struck me as being somewhat dour, with no sense of humour. In hindsight, that's what was niggling me most, because to try to create the right atmosphere and ambience of the market, I needed someone with a sense of humour.

At 7.00 a.m. next morning, as I drove to the English Market, all of this was going through my mind. The only gate open at the market was the one at Oliver Plunkett Street. Security was intense. First, I was given a printed badge, showing my name and the name of our stall. Then I had to enter through a scanner, like the one used at airports. I was searched and whatever I was carrying was checked. Again, though, the whole process was professional, efficient and courteous.

Soon, Paul arrived, followed by Liz, Denis, Emma, Seán and Kris. Normally on Fridays, we start somewhere between 6.30 and 7.00 a.m., bringing in fish, loading the counters, filleting and preparing orders. However, this particular Friday had a strange, surreal feeling about it. The fish had been brought in the previous evening, with the exception of some wild salmon which to my delight had arrived that very morning. We had no orders and no filleting, and we didn't want to fill the counters up until 11.00 a.m. to make sure that every fish looked in pristine condition. Paul, Liz, Denis, Kris and I wore our normal, cotton chefs' jackets, blue aprons, white hats and wellingtons. For Emma and Seán, we had something a little different. On the day before, we had hung the giant mural of the Sheehan family in the 1900s over our freezers at the end of the stall. To match the clothes worn by those in the photo, Emma wore a long, black dress and a white, cotton bib, while Seán dressed in a tweed cap, a waistcoat with a black back and tweed front, a collarless, striped shirt and tweed pants. To further mirror the picture, we filled old-style lobster pots with masses of seaweed and topped them off with Castletownbere's finest prawns. Also, we matched the display of white fish in the picture and decided that Emma and Seán should stand in front of the photo, with the matching display of fish before them. Everything changes and yet nothing changes.

About 11.00 a.m., we packed the main counters with ice and began to put our display together. This was very much Paul's responsibility as he has a wonderful eye for arranging fish and colour, which is probably why he is such a great photographer. My job had been to source the fish. Paul's job was to display it. Over the next few hours, under the watchful eye of Paul, everyone worked together to create a really stunning array of local, fresh fish, mostly from Castletownbere, all fit for a queen and displayed in a fashion to make the rest of the world envious of the bounty we have surrounding this island of ours – huge prawns, beautiful turbot, hake, lemon sole, plaice, mackerel, oysters, live crab and lobster, haddock, gurnard, monkfish and whiting. We topped it all off with lovely wild salmon from the River Lee and organic salmon from Bantry.

At this stage, the market was buzzing, with the stall holders fussing and double checking to make sure everything was shipshape. Bord Bia were giving advice to stall holders on final tweaks to the displays. Everywhere, cameras were flashing. The sense of anticipation was palpable. RTÉ were busy getting cameras into position, with the lighting having been put in the previous week. Security personnel were hovering around in large numbers, scrutinising every single detail.

About 1.00 p.m., RTÉ did a practice walk through the route the queen would take, to make sure that their camera angles and lighting were correct. They had to get it right as they were the feed for the other television stations showing the event and their coverage was going out worldwide. For the trial run, one of their producers, Marie Toft, picked the short straw to play the part of the queen. Accompanied by the lord mayor and several others, she followed the official route the queen would take in less than an hour. The group stopped at each of the stalls the queen would visit and tried to imitate the walk-through as best they could. Marie played the part of the queen to perfection, or at least it matched my perception of what the queen would be like – very formal, very straitlaced, aloof, without any sense of humour. If the real queen was indeed like this, my Cork wit and irreverence would go down like a lead balloon. Later, I tried to speak to one of the producers, to spell out my concerns, but it was impossible to get near any of the crew at this stage, as they were run off their feet. So, what should I do – go frightfully formal or Cork cheeky?

Paul turned on the computer. By now, the queen was being driven through the South Mall, just around the corner from the Grand Parade entrance through which she would enter the market, and the streets were thronged with people. Behind our counter, we were joined by Claire O'Sullivan of the *Irish Examiner*, P.J. Coogan from the local radio station 96FM, two photographers from England, including the royal photographer, Arthur Edwards (some of his amazing photographs are in this book), and an RTÉ camera man.

Within minutes, Queen Elizabeth II was approaching our stall, having stopped and chatted at the stall of Ashley O'Neill, the first of the seven traders selected to meet her. 'Your Majesty, *céad míle fáilte* to Cork's English Market,' says I, knowing that the queen's Irish was very good, having heard her televised speech at Dublin Castle on the previous night. Strangely enough, now I wasn't the slightest bit nervous – guess it was going to be Cork cheeky.

First, I introduced the queen to Emma and Seán and told her a little about the picture behind them. Again, I was trying to emphasise the fact that, in a place like the English Market where traditional influences are so strong, everything changes, yet nothing really changes. Then, I began to show her the huge variety of fish on display, as the two of us walked slowly down the fish aisle with the lord mayor and lady mayoress, followed by Prince Philip, Simon Coveney, Kathleen Lynch, Tim Lucey, a large entourage from City Council and an English delegation.

One of the first fish to catch the queen's eye was a large monkfish and the queen was quick to ask what it was. Now, in Cork we sometimes call this the mother-in-law fish, but this was about a week after the royal wedding of William and Kate. So, because of the person I was speaking to and because the world was looking on, and because I was in some ways representing the English Market, the city and the fish industry, I had to be diplomatic, didn't I? You must be joking, boy!

'That, Your Majesty, is what we in Cork call a mother-in-law fish.' As I said earlier, my perception of the queen was that she didn't have a great sense of humour. Boy, did I get that one wrong. She thought it was hilarious. Now Cork cheekiness was on a roll.

Next to the monkfish, Paul had arranged a gorgeous turbot. Apparently, the queen had turbot for lunch the day before in Dublin and, when I mentioned this to her, she must have wondered how I knew, but living in a small country like Ireland, word tends to travel fast. Beside the turbot lay the crème de la crème, wild salmon from our own River Lee. I took great pride in explaining to the queen that the salmon had been caught that very morning in the Lee by Simon Quilligan, a local fisherman. The salmon was in prime condition, glistening under the lights as only wild salmon can, with crimson red gills. I suppose this to me was exactly what sets the market apart as, not only could I tell the queen about the type of fish on display, but I could also say where, when and how it was caught. So there was no need to describe it as a produce of Ireland, or produced in Ireland. No, boy. This was pure Cork. The queen listened intently and seemed hugely impressed that a river running through a city the size of Cork could be clean enough to maintain such fabulous fish. Cork City Council take a bow.

While we chatted about the wild salmon, I also showed the queen organic salmon from Bantry Bay, superb in quality and appreciated all over the world. But there are big differences between wild and organic salmon, especially in relation to texture and quality.

At this stage, we were moving on to a big mound of Dublin Bay prawns, which were select prawns from one of the Castletownbere trawlers. They were absolutely massive. As I picked up several of these to show to the queen, I had a bit of a lightbulb moment myself and said, 'Your Majesty, I'll let you in on a little secret. This week, it's my thirtieth wedding anniversary and the last time I was this nervous was thirty years ago.'

'But you are all right now,' she answered, before throwing her head back in a fit of laughter. That moment was captured on camera by the photographer Valerie O'Sullivan and became one of the most iconic images of the queen's visit to Ireland – and of course ideal for the cover of this memoir!

Living the dream –
with Margaret in Garryvoe

Never realised Mam was a biker
chick until I saw this photo

Dad determined to live life to the last at the Marymount Hospice

Sheehan's Fish Stall, 1910 – an enlarged version was used to impress on the queen that in the English Market everything changes and nothing changes

Seàn, Emma, Liz, Pat, Paul, Denis and Kris minutes before the queen's visit – with Mam's picture in the background, how proud she would have been

The English Market then

The English Market today

The queen was fascinated by this guy – not me, the gunnard!

Chatting with Lord Mayor Terry Shannon about that *photo*

Discussing tactics with Presidential candidate Dana

Sharing a joke with David Norris – obviously the cod doesn't get it

Daughter Emma presenting President Mary McAleese
with a side of our smoked Irish salmon

Discussing fishing with Martin McGuinness, who is a keen angler

English Market traders take great pride in their products

Proud Dad with daughter Emma

*Margaret and myself renewing our vows on the occasion of our
25th wedding anniversary at St Michael's Church, Blackrock*

Yes!

Behind the prawns, Paul had laid some large Red Gurnard, which because of their fierce-looking head and orangey-red colour are really striking. They impressed the queen so much that she called Prince Philip closer to show them to him. We chatted for a few minutes about the gurnard before finally moving on to our own smoked salmon. Obviously, I got huge pleasure and satisfaction in telling Queen Elizabeth about our smoke-house in Bandon and it was a lovely way to end the queen's visit to our stall.

I held out my hand, we shook hands and I wished her well. Then, I sighed the biggest sigh of relief in my entire life and thought, Kathleen, we did well.

As the queen, the lord mayor and their entourage walked over towards the vegetable stall, I headed back to my staff to thank them for a job well done. Without them, the stall and the display would not have happened and I was very proud of each one of them.

Because of the large crowd, we didn't follow the queen and Prince Philip up to the Princes Street end, where they looked at the cheeses at On the Pig's Back, chatted with Isabelle Sheridan and visited Jerry Moynihan's stall, and of course where the queen received gifts at the fountain, including an English Market hamper presented by Tom Durcan, Mary Mulcahy, Daphne Landon and Mary Rose, containing a variety of foods, among them K O'Connell's smoked salmon. It was only when the group walked back down by the Chicken Inn that we were able to pick up live on the visit again. On the counter of his stall, Tim Mulcahy had day-old chicks and the queen stopped to have a look before moving on to Sheila Fitzpatrick and the

Alternative Bread Company stall, where Prince Philip was extremely tempted by Sheila's queen cakes. The Real Olive Company was the final stall on the itinerary and, as always, Toby and Jenny Rose had an impressive display of olives.

And then, the unplanned happened. On leaving the market, instead of going straight to her waiting Range Rover, the queen went across the Grand Parade and mingled freely with the crowd. It so typified the spontaneity of the Cork visit.

The visit of the queen had indeed been significant. Yet none of us could have possibly envisaged the extent of its impact.

16

The Aftermath

Before and after the queen's visit, we had been so focused on our own little world in the English Market that we had little idea about what was going on out on the streets of the city. We knew that City Council had erected large screens on Patrick Street, the Grand Parade and the South Mall to allow those on the streets to watch the visit to the market live. Yet we hadn't a clue about the atmosphere or the size of the crowds outside. We got the first hint of how large the crowds were just as the queen left the market and stepped onto the Grand Parade. It was like Páirc Uí Chaoimh on Munster final day – the crowds, the noise, the atmosphere. For many, the queen's walkabout on the Grand Parade was the icing on the cake. And one of the most wonderful pictures of that walkabout was an *Irish Examiner* front page photograph of Ross Twomey with his arms outstretched to greet the queen. As a result of that photograph, Ross became known as Royal Ross. His father Barry was a great friend of Paul and myself in Garryvoe. Just another instance of how close-knit the people of Cork are.

As the market opted to stay closed until the queen left the city centre, the traders decided to open from 4.00 p.m. to 8.00 p.m. instead. A lot of us had thought that opening for business that evening was a bit of a waste of time, but when the market did open its gates to the public, there was nothing short of a stampede. Not only that, but people were actually buying. The place was packed. It was as if Cork people had suddenly spotted this diamond in the centre of their city, which, on occasion, they had tended to take for granted.

Also, I was beginning to realise that my few minutes with the queen seemed to have made quite an impression. RTÉ, BBC, TV3, the *Irish Examiner,* 96FM, Sky News, the *Irish Independent* and the *Irish Times* all wanted interviews. For me, this was a total surprise because what I did with the queen was what I do every day of the week with all our customers. To this day, I still find the reaction surprising.

On that Friday night, all the traders closed up about 9.15 p.m. and left the market. I was absolutely shattered but happy that I had done all that was asked of me and that the queen seemed to have enjoyed the visit a lot. She had been very normal, easy to chat with, had a great sense of humour and appeared to have picked up on the Cork wit almost immediately.

When I got home, Margaret told me the market was all over the news and that the food and the place itself looked absolutely wonderful. Job well done then, I thought to myself, and fell sound asleep.

The following morning, I thought it would be business as usual, just a normal Saturday. Having arrived at work for 6.30 a.m., I started to put the counter up with Paul and the lads. Of course, all the banter centred on the previous day. At about 8.00 a.m., I headed down to the local shop to get some milk for a cup of tea. Because we are so long in business, Paul and

I would be well known in the city and there would be nothing unusual about saluting seven or eight people on the way to the shop in Oliver Plunkett Street. But this morning felt really weird, like no other. Every single person I passed was giving me a big hello, or saying, 'Well done,' or 'You did us proud.'

In the shop, as I paid for the milk, I scanned the newspapers next to the cash desk to see the headlines, as I always do. The cashier had a huge smile on her face and said laughing, 'Sick of looking at you this morning.' I could see why. That photograph of myself and the queen taken by Valerie O'Sullivan was on the front page of almost every newspaper. It was the start of everything going viral.

That Saturday, the English Market was a fascinating place to be. Although I don't have to tell this to the people of Cork, because I think everyone of them must have passed through the market at some stage on that particular day.

For weeks and months after, I received letters and cards from all over the world. Forty-odd years selling fish, and fame after four or five minutes with the queen – I must be a really poor fishmonger!

Ever since Queen Elizabeth's visit, the English Market traders have continued to see a huge surge in business. Undoubtedly, the royal visit raised the prestige of the market, put it firmly on the worldwide stage and gave it a level of publicity that money simply cannot buy. Yet, I began to wonder, could the market possibly become a victim of its own success?

17

The Risk Factor

Rick Stein, the famous chef, restaurateur and television presenter, has said that the English Market is the best covered market in the UK and Ireland combined, while restaurant reviewer Peter Calder has described it as the place where the smartest home cooks do their shopping alongside the chefs from the city's top restaurants. The market has survived wars, recessions, fires and floods. On occasion, it has been neglected by its owners. Yet, since the 1800s, it has remained at the heart of Cork's culture, character, food and economy.

Today, the market is a thriving, cosmopolitan place, busy with the best cooks, local chefs, people having lunch or a coffee and tourists. So, is everything hunky-dory then? Well, most traders would probably say so. But there are some serious concerns.

At the moment, the main issue for the traders in the English Market centres around tourism and its effect on trade in the market. But, more importantly, traders are also concerned about how certain people are trying to redefine the reason for the market's very existence. The English Market is first and foremost a local fresh food market and, to me, its very survival depends on it remaining that.

In my mind, there is absolutely no doubt that, since the visit of Queen Elizabeth II, the market has become one of the must-see places in Ireland for visitors. Isn't that great? Well, yes and no. The English Market has always boasted its fair share of tourists, and having tourists has never been a problem for the traders or local shoppers. In many ways, the presence of tourists has given the market part of that cosmopolitan feel it has today. However, one of the big problems now is the sheer volume of tourists descending on the market on any given day.

First and foremost, the English Market is a trading market. The traders depend entirely on local customers to buy their meat, vegetables, fish, poultry, cheeses or artisan food delicacies. The market's infrastructure was never designed to cater for two or three bus loads of tourists pulling up on the Grand Parade and all descending on the market together.

Today, a lot of applications for units in the market appear to be very much geared towards fast or cooked foods to cater for tourists. Up until now, the traditional traders in the market have vehemently opposed this, as they feel that such a move would dilute the traditional base of the market. Of course, it's the very tradition of the market that attracts tourists in the first place, because many of them now suddenly realise that out-of-town malls or shopping centres all tend to have a pre-packaged sameness about them. A lot of these malls and centres have become almost uniform in their design, function and choice of stores. So also, many high streets in England and elsewhere have followed the same pattern of being occupied by multiples and shops so alike that each large town and city have almost become boring replicas of each other. The market has remained steadfast in its opposition to this type of retailing, with its traders being mostly owner-occupier and deeply passionate about what they do.

Although lots of words have been written about the market, I don't think it has ever been described as bland. So, while traders have always welcomed tourists and continue to do so, there is no doubt that the huge numbers of tourists now visiting the market are a cause of great concern.

Now, more than ever, Cork City Council are well aware of the market's tourism attraction. Like any City Council with a major attraction on its doorstep, they want to maximise its potential. Recently, we have heard much talk of either incorporating nearby buildings into the market, or adding a food innovation centre to the market, or beside it.

While the traders of the market are not against change or investment to the area next to the market, many are wary of the ideas being floated around and the lack of consistent engagement with the traders or their representatives. The market is not broken. Do not try to fix it. By all means enhance it and its surrounding areas, but do not dilute its tradition, character or produce. Today, the market stands as a prime example of being one of the best, living, working, thriving markets in Europe. Do nothing to upset that fine balance. Future generations will not thank you.

Naturally, being a member of various market traders' committees down through the years, I've had many an argument with City Council officials over service, charges and rents. The council is obliged to maximise income from the market. As traders, we want to ensure that the market remains much as it is and that small traders working long hours, particularly in winter, often in uncomfortable conditions, can make a reasonable return on their business without being crippled by rents.

For the most part, the traders' committee have found City Council officials to be understanding of the economic realities of the market and appreciative of the market's immense value to the city. To date, the council have invested heavily in the market. On the whole, relations between council officials and the traders have always been excellent. However, particularly during the Celtic Tiger era, there have been times when Cork City Council officials have attempted to compare rents of Patrick Street – Cork's main shopping street – with those of the market. You may as well be comparing chalk with cheese. But on many occasions during these discussions, I began to wonder was it a given that everyone these days understood there was a difference between chalk and cheese. If rents equal to those charged on shops on Patrick Street, or anything remotely near them, were ever imposed on the English Market then we might as well knock the place down and build a multi-storey car park there instead. It would be much more reassuring to the traders if some general parameters were put in place rather than having to constantly worry about which council officials have charge of the market portfolio, and how familiar they are with the way in which the market works.

Going forward, it's vital for the success of the market that everyone involved understands its strengths and its frailties. Otherwise, there will always be a risk. On rents alone, the market will never be of major value to the council. Its value lies totally in the sum of its parts.

18

A Magical Place

For me, Christmas in the English Market is something special. At that particular time of year, the market emanates
a heightened sense of tradition, pride in its produce, a feeling
of warmth, even on the coldest December day, and an air of
homeliness too that I have never seen or sensed anywhere else.

At all times, the English Market epitomises quality food,
but even more so at Christmas, with turkeys hanging from the
Chicken Inn, Moynihan's, Landon's and many of the butchers, and the aroma of the spiced beef from Durcan's, Boylan's,
O'Neill's, O'Mahony's, Bresnan's and Paul Murphy's, and our
own stall, heaving with fresh Dublin Bay prawns, mussels, oysters and smoked organic Irish salmon from our own artisan
smokehouse in West Cork.

Every day, we try to be the best at what we do and strive to
improve the way we do things and the service we provide. It's
something that has been engrained into us from an early age
and also something that I have tried to impress on my own
children. If you do your best, that is all anyone can ask of you.

At Christmas, the pressure tends to be intense. It's the one
time of the year when everyone wants the perfect meal. If possible, we make sure not to let down the fish side of things. How-

ever, as fish is so perishable and because the fish industry is so weather-dependent, there are times when we get stretched to the limit. But I think there has yet to be a Christmas when we have let anybody down, or when we have failed to deliver the best of Irish fish.

Usually, November and December tend to go by in a blur, what with taking orders for prawns, salmon and smoked salmon, both for our local and international customers, our feet rarely seem to touch the ground for about six weeks. The strange thing is that everyone in the market gets caught up in the buzz and atmosphere and the enthusiasm never seems to wane.

Then, all of a sudden, around 4.00 p.m. on Christmas eve, it's like somebody switches off a light. The crowds quickly disperse, stall holders tidy up in haste and within thirty minutes the market becomes eerily quiet, deserted.

I'm always the last one to leave, as we usually close for three days at Christmas and I like to make sure that everything is put neatly away and that the stall is spotless. After all the hustle and bustle of the previous few weeks, I always find it strange that the market can become so calm and almost ghostly in the space of an hour.

Having spent fifty years of my life involved with the market, I quickly find myself reminiscing about Christmases past. I think of the Bagnalls, the Sheehans, the O'Sullivans, the Mc-Donnells, the Mulcahys, the Ahernes and the Rileys, people who would have been so much part of the market and are now no longer there. Once more, I get that feeling that everything changes, yet nothing changes. And I picture myself as a child again, raising myself up on my toes at our front window and bursting with pride at the sight of Dad driving a big dumper. As clear as daylight, I see myself standing beside Mam, carefully loading boxes of fish on to a long, narrow trolley belonging to Clayton Love, then pushing the trolley together down the Grand Parade and across the road, struggling to keep the boxes in place, then hacking back if we failed to mount the kerb and trying again. And then, I spot tiny Georgie Bear lugging a massive side of beef on his shoulders and I hear the constant pounding of a ball in the alley, where Paul and I used to play with our friend Kevin.

As my thoughts drift slowly away from the past, I begin to wonder. What does the future hold? In fifty years' time, will somebody else stand where I stand now and reminisce as I do? And will their name be O'Connell? I feel optimistic that it will. And I hope that whoever stands behind the counter will have as much passion about fish and about the market as Paul and myself and our mother, and that they will get as much fun and pleasure out of what they do as we do now. The English Market – it truly is a magical place.

With my heart filled with hope for the future, I give the counter one last polish. To the sound of my own footsteps, I walk briskly through the market gates and out into the crisp, December air. Then I hop on my bike and happily head for home with the Christmas lights of the city gleaming brightly overhead.

Acknowledgements

Sometime early in 2013, I got a phone call on a Friday morning from a woman I didn't know. Patricia Ahern told me she was an author and had recently co-written a book called *The Lightkeeper*. All very interesting, but what had that to do with me? Her next question took the wind out of my sails – would I be interested in putting my life story in print? My first reaction was, this has to be a wind-up, why would anyone want to read a book about a fishmonger? I needed time to suss this out, so I said, as it was Friday and we were busy, would she mind ringing me back on Tuesday. That weekend, I called into Waterstones book store and sure enough Patricia Ahern is very much an author. But why would she want me to put my story in writing? I didn't open our business, I certainly don't feel in any great way responsible for its success, which was very much down to a woman called Kathleen O'Connell, my mother. And that's when I decided the answer would be yes. So, although my name is on the cover, this book is very much about my mother and my family. To Trish, I say a very big thank you for your ever so gentle persuasion, for the huge amount of time you gave me on teasing out a story, and for the opportunity you have given me to speak about the wonderful parents that Paul and I had. Patricia Ahern, a very serious thank you.

There are forty-four traders in the market. Most we get on extremely well with, some we don't get on with at all, and that's okay, that's human nature and that's competition. But together we give the market its character and its sense of Cork and, for that, every trader should take a bow. The sum of the English Market is greater than any of its parts.

Rebecca Harte is intelligent, attractive, sometimes a little shy in the public arena, but it has been amazing to see Rebecca grow into her job in the Farmgate under the tutelage of her mother Kay. What a team and what an asset to the market. Rebecca, thank you for the ego-boosting foreword.

Valerie O'Sullivan is the Kerry lass responsible for the iconic photo of Queen Elizabeth II and me that appears on the cover. A nicer, more down-to-earth girl you will never meet. What a lady, what a photographer. And she's in fabulous company here with photos from Arthur Edwards, MBE, and Tony O'Connell.

Speaking of photographers, the lads in the *Irish Examiner* and *Evening Echo* deserve a very special mention. Down through the years, they have chronicled the life of the English Market through their lens. Their work has been of the very highest standard. The *Examiner* office has, like the English Market, become a Cork institution, so a very sincere thank you to Brian Lougheed and his staff, not only from Paul and myself but I think from everyone in the market.

These days, our public service tends to get a slating from all sides. Yet my experience of City Council officials, the gardaí, the fire service, Bord Fáilte and Bord Bia in the lead-up to and during the visit of Queen Elizabeth II was one of utmost courtesy, efficiency and professionalism that any country would be proud of. That visit of course led to contact with our own Department of Foreign Affairs, the British Embassy and Buckingham Palace staff, from all of them we received nothing but the utmost courtesy.

I also want to thank Mary Lenihan for proofreading the text and for her recommendations; authors Diarmuid and Donal Ó Drisceoil, whose wonderful book *Serving a City* proved a valuable source of reference, especially in relation to the history of the market; the Department of Foreign Affairs for granting copyright permission to use the front cover photo; and the *Irish Examiner* and *Evening Echo* for copyright permission to use previously published pictures.

But of course it's those closest to me I must particularly thank: my brother Paul, his wife Marian and sons Seán and Eoin; my wife Margaret and daughters Sarah and Emma; and our present and past staff. These are the people who have made the most sacrifice in time, dedication and effort in maintaining the legacy of my mother Kathleen. I sincerely thank all of you from the bottom of my heart.

All royalties paid to Pat O'Connell in respect of this book will be donated to Marymount University Hospice Cork.